ZENITH

The 17th (Northern) Division on the Somme August – December 1916

Wayne Osborne

Salient Books

British Library Cataloguing In Publication Data

A Record of this Publication is available from the British Library

ISBN 978-0-9574459-9-4

First Published 2018 by

Salient Books,
21, Collington Street, Beeston, Nottingham, NG9 1FJ

www.salientbooks.co.uk

Cover Design © H.Osborne at Salient Books 2018

Cover Image ©IWM(Q 1615)
Troops Returning from the Trenches near Bernafay Wood,
November 1916; Photography Lt Ernest Brooks

*To Major-General Philip R. Robertson
and his "splendid Division."*

Contents

Maps

Acknowledgements

I would like to thank Helen and Abigail Osborne, John Bourne, Pete Simkins, Jim Grundy, John Dandy, Mark Barnes, Warren Osborne, Dave Edwards, Morris Eddison, Steve Erskine at the Green Howards Museum, the staff at The National Archives and the staff at The Imperial War Museum.

Author's Note

I stood in the impressive gateway of Pozieres cemetery, a long time ago now, and alone, looked out across the ranks of headstones which were presenting their names, numbers, units, epitaphs and Unknowns. It was here that I decided that I would write about the Somme Campaign. There were so many untold stories of ordinary people lying there and across the Somme battlefield that I had a sudden desire to find out about what had really happened and write about some of their story. By the time that I returned to my friend John Dandy, who was scouting around for signs of old trenches the idea had taken a firm hold.

So I did, focusing initially on one man whom I believed to be a relative and who turned out not to be. Then the work expanded to encompass research into the 17th (Northern) Division's service on the Somme in 1916. A number of visits (sometimes weekly) to the Somme followed with John, my brother Warren and Dave Edwards among others and I paced the ground in all weathers trying to visualise that Campaign from ground level. That moment at Pozieres was a life changing one, after it, using the war diaries and unpublished works, I researched, wrote and published *Quadrangles*, *Delville Wood* and this volume, *Zenith*; a trilogy about the 17th Division in the Somme Campaign. A number of other books followed as did my MA under the tutelage of John Bourne, Peter Simkins and Gary Sheffield; then my PhD with Keith Case and his Engineers. It led me to Gallipoli with Jim Grundy, Mark Barnes and Peter Hart and the production of another book, *Suvla 15*. It was quite a ride, really.

It has become a movement to grumble about the waves of Somme books, about how weary one has become of them. I sympathise, but we don't have to read everything that comes out do we? Over the years, being one of those who has added to the pile of Somme Campaign books, I have come to the conclusion that people *should* write books about the Somme and long may the Somme live in the collective memory. The Somme Campaign is not the preserve of academics or a select few. The memory belongs to the people of the nations who were there, to the ordinary people who made the history of the campaign and to those who wish to research or simply find out what happened.

Having completed this, the third book in the trilogy, I have realised that I am one of the many and am no longer the lone figure at the gates. It has taken a long time to finish this work because other books, life in general and, most importantly, my daughter's continuing recovery from Leukaemia have taken my time. Nonetheless, 'tis done' and the Somme Campaign has had another window opened. Like the others before us; soldiers of both sides, historians, locals and visitors; one way or another we have all become part of the Somme. Everyone has the right to research and write about the Somme if they wish and *no one* has the right to say that they cannot.

Wayne Osborne. Nottingham, 2017.

Maps

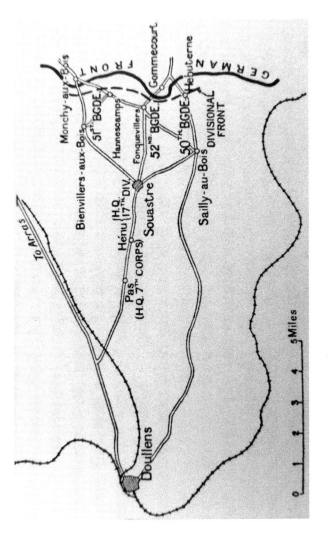

Gommecourt Salient 1916.
From Atteridge, History of the 17th (Northern) Division, p. 163

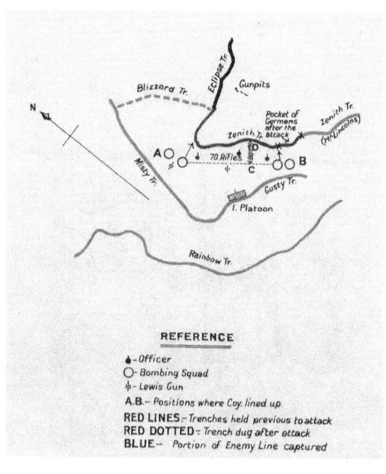

Blizzard Tr.   Eclipse Tr.   Gunpits

Zenith Tr. (7th Lincolns)

Pocket of
Germans
after the
attack

Zenith Tr.

A   70.Rifles   D   B
C

Misty Tr.

Gusty Tr.

I. Platoon

Rainbow Tr.

N

REFERENCE

♠ - *Officer*
○ - *Bombing Squad*
⫯ - *Lewis Gun*
A.B.- *Positions where Coy. lined up.*
RED LINES - *Trenches held previous to attack*
RED DOTTED = *Trench dug after attack*
BLUE - *Portion of Enemy Line captured*

Map of the attack upon Zenith Trench; more than likely made after the operation.
From TNA: PRO. WO 95/1918. War Diary, 17th Division, November 1916.

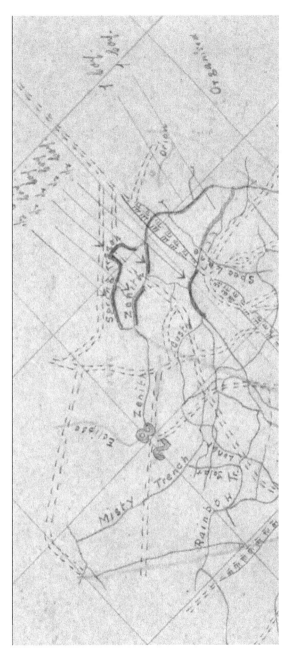

Hand traced map of Zenith Trench
From TNA: PRO. WO 95/1918. War Diary, 17th Division, November 1916.

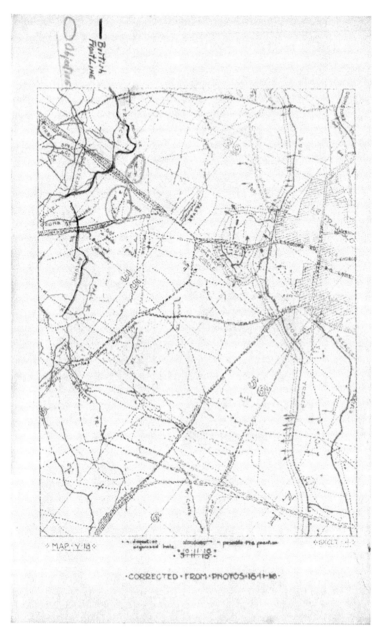

Map of the Le Transloy Sector showing front lines and no-man's-land
From TNA: PRO. WO 95/1981. War Diary, 17th Division, November 1916.

Taking of Zenith Trench
A Dramatic Story

A news story in an Australian newspaper on 9 November 1916, the day that the official narrative of the operation was published in Fourth Army, citing the Reuters network as the source, said,

> It was a dark night ... and an officer went out to reconnoitre. He was absent a long time, but he eventually returned, shouldering a machine gun. It appears that he crept up to the German parapet and swung himself over very stealthily. He found that the sentries were considerably apart and inattentive. The officer detached a machine gun unobserved, clambered out of the trench and got home safely.

> The discovery that the enemy was not on the qui vive led to an immediate and successful attack upon Zenith Trench. We had only a dozen casualties.[1]

A stirring story and one to cheer the allied readership at breakfast in November 1916; but was it true? What happened in the 17th Division's sector opposite Le Transloy in the dying days of the Somme Campaign? Surely, it was not that simple? No, it was not.

---

[1] *Bendigonian (Bendigo, Vic, 1914 – 18)*. Thursday 9 November 1916, p. 23. Thanks to Jim Grundy.

Up at Gommecourt and then South to The Somme

When the 17th (Northern) Division left Delville Wood the units went to Buire Camp on the River Ancre and from there they moved to a rest area to the south-west of Doullens and came under the command of General Sir Edmund Allenby's Third Army. On 18 August the 17th Division was ordered by General Sir Thomas D'Oyly Snow's[2] VII Corps to move to the line east of Doullens and take over there from the 56th Division.[3] Their new sector was a four mile long stretch of line with its centre opposite the German held Gommecourt Salient. To the right was Hébuterne and opposite the left flank of the line was Monchy-aux-Bois.[4] It was here on 1 July 1916, during a diversionary attack for the main thrust on the Somme, that the 46th and 56th Divisions fared so badly.

In August 1916, the Gommecourt Salient was a genuinely quiet sector and a fairly wide no-man's-land, 1,000 yards in places, divided the lines.[5] Indeed, for a number of days at the end of August the 17th Division war diary recorded, "Division in the

---

2   Known variously as "Slush", "Snowball" or "Polar Bear." *General's Nicknames.* University of Birmingham.

3   TNA: PRO. WO 95/1981. War Diary, 17th Division, August, 1916.

4   A. Hilliard Atteridge, *History of the 17th (Northern) Division,* (Robert Maclehose & Co. Ltd, 1929), p. 162.

5   W. N. Hoyte, M. T. F. J. McNeela (Ed), *10th (S) Battalion The Sherwood Foresters, The History Of The Battalion During The Great War,* (Originally written shortly after the war's end, at the request of a number of 10th Battalion Officers, by William Norman Hoyte during a summer break on the north coast of Scotland before he returned to his studies at Cambridge. It was not published until Mr. McNeela edited the manuscript and brought it to the attention of Naval & Military Press. First published, Naval & Military Press, 2003), p. 19

line. No events of importance to record."[6] It was a welcome respite after Quadrangle Support Trench and Delville Wood. Lieutenant William Norman Hoyte,[7] a former 10th Notts & Derbys officer and an officer on the 51st Brigade Staff, wrote, "After the unending racket of Caterpillar Valley and Delville Wood it seemed after all that life might be worth living."[8] Some rear trenches were in good condition, there was minimal shelling, a few locals still lived in their intact villages and there was even a complete country house, the Château de la Haye, lying between Fonquevillers and Souastre. Standing empty on the sky line it was only 4,000 yards from the German batteries at Gommecourt Wood. Minus many windows but complete with stables the house and buildings were soon commandeered as Brigadier-General John Louis Justice Clarke's[9] 52nd Brigade H.Q. The British 56th Divisional artillery stood nearby and comments were made by brigade staff officers on how remarkable it was that the house and buildings had survived relatively unscathed. Two days later the British were shelled out of the Château by the German gunners, who had registered the General's presence. Brigadier-General Clarke and his staff were forced to take refuge in a house in the nearby town of Souastre.[10]

---

6   TNA: PRO. WO 95/1981. War Diary, 17th Division, August, 1916.

7   Hoyte arrived on the Western Front on 15 July 1915 as a second lieutenant. He was promoted to lieutenant and soon joined the 51st Brigade staff and after a time as bombing officer he became the brigade's intelligence officer, despite a stint on loan to the 52nd Brigade it was a post that he held for the rest of the war. He was awarded the M.C. in 1917. He acted with great bravery at Amerval when the 51st Brigade came under attack. The situation was 'obscure' and he went forward to gather information. Hoyte found a leaderless company of the 7th Borders who had been forced out of their position, taking command, he rallied the company and led them into action on the right flank of the 51st Brigade and checked the German attack.

8   Hoyte, *10th (S) Battalion*, p. 19

9   Clarke arrived on the Western Front as a Major in the East Yorkshire Regiment on 8 September 1914 although his Medal Index Card also shows a disembarkation date of 14 October 1914. He was promoted to Lieutenant-Colonel and then Brigadier-General. He took command of the 52nd Brigade in March 1916.

10   Atteridge, *History of the 17th (Northern) Division*, p. 164.

Set in a hollow, Souastre had avoided much of the shell fire that had been meted out in the last two years of war and the inhabitants were still there, making a living off the British units and H.Qs that had set up there. Workshops, canteens, estaminet and shops and even an improvised theatre[11] all played their parts in this H.Q. town. In fact, the 17th Division's theatrical and concert troupe, "The Duds," gave their first performance at the theatre on 6 September with Major-General Philip Rynd Robertson,[12] the 17th Divisional G.O.C., in attendance as the guest of honour.[13]

Captain Geoffrey O'Hanlon, M.C.,[14] an officer in Lieutenant-Colonel Cecil A. Rowley's[15] 6th Dorsets, was bullish in his descriptions of this sector, claiming that his battalion treated the front line and no-man's-land "with hilarious disrespect." There was fruit to be picked and honey to be found. Apart from the rats the front line was almost luxurious, he wrote and "the enemy line was a long way off, and was reputed to be held by one man, a boy and a dog." He cited a certain Second Lieutenant Eric K. A. Boyce,[16] the battalion's irrepressible Regimental Bombing Officer, who claimed and proved that people took tea between the lines by returning from patrol with a piece of crockery. Boyce suggested to battalion H.Q. that the Germans on the other side needed stirring up and recommended that the battalion band be sent into no-man's-land to practice. In

---

[11] A former barn.

[12] Robertson arrived on the Western Front as the Lieutenant-Colonel of the 1st Cameronians, the Scottish Rifles, the on 15 August 1914. He was promoted to Major-General and took command of the 17th Division in July 1916.

[13] Atteridge, *History of the 17th (Northern) Division*, p. 165.

[14] Captain O'Hanlon, a former school teacher, had been with the 6th Dorsets since the battalion's formation in September 1914 and had gone out to France and Flanders on 13 July 1915.

[15] Lieutenant-Colonel Cecil Rowley D.S.O., had been with the 6th Dorsets since the battalion's formation in Dorset in 1914; he was highly regarded by his officers and men who looked upon him as a father figure. He led the battalion to the Western Front on 13 July 1915.

[16] Eric Boyce may well be the officer later referred to as 'Blitz' by Captain B. C. Mozley.

response to this tactical suggestion H.Q. ordered him to reconnoitre the enemy wire after an artillery bombardment. Boyce went out as ordered and on his return sent two envelopes to H.Q. One, containing a sample of wire, was marked "Herewith sample of wire." The other, marked "Herewith sample of gap," contained nothing.[17] His humour was much appreciated by his comrades and the general holiday mood, brought on by late summer and the absence of offensive operations and general destruction, was not surprising after the grim experiences of July and August on the Somme. Lieutenant Hoyte agreed and wrote that at Gommecourt in August and September, "The whole operation seemed to be absolutely playing at war …"[18]

Lieutenant-Colonel Ronald D'Arcy Fife[19] the C.O., of the 7th Yorks did not think so and his tone in his diary for September was depressed and there was no hint of cheer in his writing. He recalled men being hit by stray rounds and fitful shelling by the enemy, the weather was poor and wet and the billets were dirty and infested with flies. He also recorded that he was ill, shivery and rheumatic and it was the real reason for his miserable diary entries. Fife was indeed ill and exhausted after his recent experiences in the Somme Campaign and on 29 August he was sent home on leave for five days.[20] His battalion's war diary, on the other hand and in common with other diaries and memoires,

---

17 G. O' Hanlon, *A Plain History of the Sixth (Service) Battalion, The Dorsetshire Regiment 1914 – 1919, in The History of the Dorsetshire Regiment 1914 – 1919. Part three, the Service Battalions.* (First published, Henry Ling, Ltd, 1932. Re-printed by Naval & Military Press), p. 123

18 Hoyte, *10th (S) Battalion* p. 19

19 A reserve officer, Lieutenant-Colonel Fife, C.M.G., D.S.O., had been in command of his battalion since its formation at Richmond in 1914. Fife may well have been susceptible to illness and took a number of leaves during his time in command. There was no doubting his courage, he was Mentioned in Despatches four times; on 1 January 1916, 15 June 1916, 4 January 1917 and 22 May 1917, and his ability as a battalion commander was in no doubt, he also commanded the 50th Brigade when the Brigadier-General was on leave.

20 Personal diary of Lieutenant-Colonel Fife held at the Green Howards Museum, Richmond.

painted a peaceful picture. Recording that the only casualties were woundings. On 20 August the entry read, "Very quiet by day and night. A few shells into the village [Heberturne] during the day & a certain amount of machine gun fire at night. Working parties by day improving trenches and by night wiring in front of advanced posts."[21] And it was the same on the other side of the line; 23 August, "The Germans are doing a good deal of work on their line & front trenches at night"[22] and, by and large, they were allowed to get on with it with the minimum of interference. The line was quiet and the British and the Germans got on, relatively unmolested, with their respective consolidation work.[23]

Another 6th Dorset's officer, A Company Commander, Captain Bernard Charles Mozley, D.S.O.,[24] recalled the Gommecourt Salient and their arrival at the village of Sailly. The war seemed to have forgotten Gommecourt,

The Company was put up in old gun pits close to the road through the village, while the officers found good billets in a house nearby. Two other companies were billeted in the same street, while the remaining one went on to Hébuterne. The next morning I accompanied Shaw in a tour of inspection of the defences between Sailly and Hébuterne. We found these to consist chiefly of wire, with very little in the way of trenches anywhere, those trenches that we did discover were mostly fallen in and overgrown with rubbish.[25]

Chief among the duties here in the line facing Gommecourt, apart from training, was consolidation and reconstruction of the

21 TNA: PRO. WO 95/2004. War Diary, 7th Yorks, September, 1916.
22 TNA: PRO. WO 95/2004. War Diary, 7th Yorks, September, 1916.
23 TNA: PRO. WO 95/2004. War Diary, 7th Yorks, September, 1916.
24 Captain Mozley, commissioned on 20 September 1914, had been with the 6th Dorsets since they had formed and went out to France and Flanders on 14 July 1915. He was awarded the D.S.O and earned a Mention in Despatches after, despite being wounded himself, carrying the wounded Lieutenant Brown back into British lines in February 1916.
25 Imperial War Museum (IWM): Unpublished papers Captain B. C. Mozley, D.S.O. 01/48/1.

line after the heavy fighting in July. An entry in a VII Corps weekly operation report for the end of August said,

> *Work has been continued throughout the week on communication trenches, support and fire trenches, and the making of deep dug outs in preparation for the winter. Wire has also been strengthened at several points, and considerable progress has been made towards the consolidation of the reclaimed portions of the front line.*[26]

Captain Mozley recorded something of the work that the men of the 17th Division did while they were at Gommecourt and what had happened in the early days of July 1916 was not far from the soldier's minds.

> *It should be mentioned that the attacks on the Hébuterne front in July ended in failure, the German machine gunners being backed up by a very heavy concentration of guns, which wrought great havoc in the original British front line. This front trench was in some places so smashed in and flattened, that it was only held at night by isolated posts, and a tremendous amount of work had to be put through here, in order that the trenches should be restored to something like their previous condition. The R.E. of course were continually in the line, supervising the work. There was also a large quantity of bombs, S.A.A. and stores of all kinds, which had to be salvaged…*[27]

Lieutenant Hoyte wrote about the part of the line between Fonquevillers and Hannes camps; there was plenty of evidence of the 1 July fighting there as well.

> *This spot had seen some of the most determined fighting on July 1st when Gommecourt was attacked. Traces were still to be seen – No Man's Land was a mass of shallow assembly trenches, and the forward positions of the enemy showed signs of the tremendous bombardment to which they had been subjected. But there was practically no enemy activity.*[28]

---

[26] TNA: PRO. WO 95/805. War Diary, VII Corps, August, 1916.

[27] IWM: Mozley, 01/48/1.

[28] Hoyte, *10th (S) Battalion*, p. 19

There was some shelling and sporadic firing but as Hoyte had noted the sector remained in the main quiet and the work progressed well. Night time patrols were allowed to roam free and more often than not returned with nothing worth reporting. Working parties went out nightly to improve the wire and defences. Captain Mozley recalled one night, after "a little refreshment"[29] when he, Captain O'Hanlon and an officer nicknamed 'Blitz'[30] ventured out into no-man's-land to see how their working parties were getting on. A machine gun suddenly opened fire away on the left and 'Blitz' was so startled that he nearly fell into a shell hole; this delighted Mozley and O'Hanlon and they dissolved into a fit of giggles while 'Blitz' was indignantly, and loudly, vocal about the whole affair. Captain Mozley wrote, "The wiring parties were probably very glad when we withdrew."[31] Such was the peaceful nature of no-man's-land that they received no attention at all.

Despite the evident humour in these recollections and memoirs; the dead, who lay strewn around the Salient and who also had to be cleared away and buried, were edited out save for a small note by Captain O'Hanlon. He wrote briefly that the work in the trenches was, "a melancholy business, as there were many dead bodies…"[32]

Nonetheless, this sector seems to have stuck in the memories of the survivors and was remembered like an oasis in the desert. This did not mean that soldiers did not die here. On their way into the sector on the evening of 20 August the 6th Dorsets witnessed the death of an observer who fell from a drifting balloon. Captain Mozley wrote that they saw a German scout attacking the British observation balloon; it burst into flames and one of the observers successfully parachuted to safety. The

---

[29] Captain Mozley was at pains to point out that the refreshment was cocoa but he did not say what was in the cocoa.

[30] Possibly Eric Boyce the Bombing Officer.

[31] IWM: Mozley, 01/48/1.

[32] O'Hanlon, *A Plain History of the Sixth (Service) Battalion*, p. 123

other man clung to the basket until his grip loosened and he fell to his death, his parachute failing to deploy. This man was Captain Basil Hallam Radford of the R.F.C., formerly a famous entertainer known for his character 'Gilbert the Filbert'.[33] Shells, while not being fired in anything like the volume that were being fired further south, still brought random death and destruction. Second Lieutenant Hugh Joseph Fleming,[34] who had been with the 6th Dorsets for just two days, was killed in the street in Hébuterne by a shell on 24 August 1916.[35] Consolidation work and training went on.

So it continued, in the opinion of the survivors of the war, *not* latter day historians, the peaceful, quiet sector presented "trench warfare of the dullest, most workaday type."[36] It might have been, but the work that the 17th Division troops were doing, clearing, rebuilding, wiring, salvaging and burying was in order to pave the way for a new offensive at Gommecourt.

An experimental gas attack was prepared, and this unpredictable weapon was brought in cylinders up to the front line.[37] The front line infantry were not at all keen on gas even if it was used by their own side but the staff planners seemed to have a different view. Captain Mozley wrote, "… division seemed fond of making experimental gas attacks."[38] Lieutenant Hoyte recalled that the 10th Notts & Derbys were not very happy to have gas cylinders in their trenches, "No work or digging was

---

[33] IWM: Mozley, 01/48/1. & O' Hanlon, *A Plain History of the Sixth (Service) Battalion*, p. 123. & the Commonwealth War Graves Commission. Rudyard Kipling gave a slightly different account of Radford's death in his book, *The Irish Guards in the Great War, Volume II, Salient and the Somme.* Kipling's account mentions no scout aeroplane but does say that the balloon had become untethered as it was being hauled down and had drifted towards the German lines. Kipling then stated that Radford's body fell some 3,000 feet and landed near a British Brigade H.Q.

[34] Fleming had been seconded from the 7th Dorsets and had only arrived in France seven days before on 17 August 1916.

[35] O'Hanlon, *A Plain History of the Sixth (Service) Battalion,* p. 123. & the Commonwealth War Graves Commission.

[36] Hoyte, *10th (S) Battalion*, p. 20

[37] Atteridge, *History of the 17th (Northern) Division*, p. 166

[38] IWM: Mozley, 01/48/1.

allowed to take place near them, and an enormous amount of wires in code had to be sent about the creatures every day."[39] It was not Divisional H.Q. that was keen on experimenting with gas, nor was it General Snow's VII Corps. It was Third Army, which had been ordering the gas attacks in the Gommecourt Sector since August.[40]

On 6 September with a favourable wind the gas was released into the German trenches. It wafted over the German front line and blew into the German gun line. Panic gripped the German infantry and gunners, rockets and lights were fired and the German guns began to fire. The gas affected the gunners and, in the opinion of their British counterparts who were observing with interest, their bombardment of the British lines and barrage fire was sporadic and feeble. The guns, covering the 17th Division in the line opened counter-battery fire but when it was obvious that no infantry attack was developing the sector calmed down and returned to its usual, soporific state.[41]

It took about 1 ¾ minutes [for the gas] to reach the German trenches. As the gas reached them the German infantry fired numerous Verey lights and flares, the latter bursting into two red stars. Other flares seen further behind the German lines burst into two green stars. British intelligence decided that some of these lights were S.O.S signals to the artillery. The German troops in the front line opened fire on the British line with rifles and two machine guns. Lieutenant-Colonel Metcalfe of the 7th Lincolns reported to Brigadier-General Trotter that the rifle fire was weak and wild, some rounds passing twenty feet above the roof tops of Foncquevillers. The two machine guns fired spasmodically and it was believed by the men in the front line that both weapons kept jamming. No gas gongs or other auditory alarm signals were heard. The German

---

[39] Hoyte, *10th (S) Battalion*, p. 20

[40] TNA: PRO. WO 95/360. War Diary, Third Army, August, 1916.

[41] TNA: PRO. WO 95/1981. War Diary, 17th Division, September, 1916 & Atteridge, *History of the 17th (Northern) Division*, p. 166. Atteridge states that the gas attack was launched on 7 September but the date given by the divisional war diary was 6 September. To confuse matters, VII Corps gives the date as 5 September… Aris and Griffith are recorded as being killed on 5 September 1916.

trench mortars also opened fire. If the flares were S.O.S signals then the artillery response was poor. The firing was slow, wild and not very well aimed. Only one shell hit the Lincolns front line trench. It blew up two fire bays and killed two of the Special Engineers who operated the cylinders, Pioneers Sidney Aris and John Griffith. There was no attempt at barrage fire by the German guns and although shells landed around the British positions there did not seem, to the men in the line, that there were any specifically targeted British areas. By 9.00 pm the line had calmed down and returned to normal apart from some desultory mortar fire.

A patrol of the 10th Lancashires was sent out under Second Lieutenant Haworth to assess the situation in in no man's land. The gas was seemingly clear up to 150 yards of the British front lines though it was seen to hang over Gommecourt Park. When Haworth's patrol reached the German wire the men began to feel the effects of the gas. Then Haworth and one of his men fell into a shell hole and of course this was full of gas. They were very badly gassed as were the men who pulled them out of the hole. Desultory mortar fire ceased at 11.30 am and that seemed to be about it. The British did not launch an attack and were satisfied to watch the effects of the gas discharge on the German line.

On 9 September the 7th Borders were ordered to provide ten carrying parties to 'O' Company of the 4th Battalion, Special Brigade. These men of the Special Brigade looked after the gas cylinders that lurked in the right hand sector. The carrying parties each consisting of one officer, four N.C.Os and 40 men were to report to a dump behind the lines, manned by the Special Brigade, pile all equipment and weapons and received the issue of one empty sand bag each. Then each party, led by a guide from the Special Brigade, would then proceed along a preset route guarded by trench wardens and watched over by regimental police provided by the 7th Lincolns. No one else would be using this route and the parties had to travel in total silence. Their Special Brigade guides led the parties to the right sector where the 200 gas cylinders lay. Each party was to carry twenty cylinders on their shoulders out of the line. The sand bag was the only padding provided. Once a party had its allotment of cylinders, it would leave along another route similarly guarded and in silence. The cylinders were taken back to the dump where lorries waited to whisk them away. The work was hard and the going difficult. The carrying parties did not manage to remove all of the cylinders during the day. The carrying parties completed their task and the last of the gas cylinders left the sector on the following day.[42]

Third Army had issued orders for an attack upon the Gommecourt Salient and on 9 September orders arrived from General Snow at Corps H.Q., for Major-General Robertson and his staff to make and submit a plan for the operation.

Orders received from VIIth [sic] Corps to prepare plans for an attack on German trenches immediately south of Gommecourt Park and opposite W Sector; the 33rd Div. attacking on the left 17th Div. and the Reserve Army on the right. The attack to be made on a two brigade front. First objective the two front lines of enemy trenches. The ridge NAMELESS FARM – CEMETERY. Second objective not to be attempted until 33rd Div. has established itself in Gommecourt Park. Wire cutting by artillery to be commenced at once. The attack to be made on 20th Sept. if ordered.[43]

Corps recorded that, "the attack will be made in conjunction with an attack by the Reserve Army from the south in the direction of Achiet le Grand and Achiet le Petit. In order to assist the attack of the Reserve Army extensive counter battery work will have to be done …"[44] General Snow went on to ask what artillery and ammunition was needed for the attack. Gun emplacements had already been constructed in anticipation of the renewed attack on Gommecourt.[45]

---

[42]   TNA: PRO. WO 95/2008. War Diary, 7th Borders, September 1916. TNA: PRO. WO 95/2007. War Diary, 7th Lincolns, September, 1916. TNA: PRO. WO95/2012. War Diary, 10th Lancashire Fusiliers, September 1916. in W. Osborne, *A History Of The 10th Battalion The Notts & Derbys, Volume Two, The Bluff To The Somme 1916.* (First published, Salient Books, 2011), p. 265 – 6.

[43]   TNA: PRO. WO 95/1981. War Diary, 17th Division, September, 1916.

[44]   TNA: PRO. WO 95/805. War Diary, VII Corps, September, 1916.

[45]   TNA: PRO. WO 95/805. War Diary, VII Corps, September, 1916.

The artillery planners' response was swift and soon heavy batteries began to arrive from VI Corps to augment the Divisional artillery in preparation for the attack on the Gommecourt Salient and to provide counter-battery fire in support of the Reserve Army operations.[46] The artillery support proposed for the attack was not inconsiderable. Seventy-nine 6-inch and 15-inch howitzers with an allotment of 90,000 rounds. Forty-eight 4.7-inch and 6-inch guns with 48,000 rounds. Eight 240 mm Trench Mortars with 1,200 rounds. Twenty-eight 4.5-inch Howitzers with 50,000 rounds and 114 18-pounders with 350,000 rounds and 10,000 gas shells (recorded in the 17th Division diary as 'lethal shells').[47] On 14 September a 12-inch howitzer on a railway mounting joined VII Corps from Second Army.[48] Ammunition allotments and supply were no longer a problem for the British, as they had been in 1915, thanks to the increasing ramp up of munitions production back home.

Corps informed Third Army that in August a series of tunnels had been begun going out from the British front line, under no-man's-land towards the German front. The plan being that they could be used for communication between the two lines once the German trenches were in British hands. They had not yet reached the German line but the work was continuing, apparently undetected.[49]

On 11 September Major-General Robertson ordered Brigadier-General William James Theodore Glasgow,[50] 50th Brigade and Brigadier-General Gerald Frederick Trotter,[51] 51st Brigade to

---

46   TNA: PRO. WO 95/805. War Diary, VII Corps, September, 1916.

47   TNA: PRO. WO 95/1981. War Diary, 17th Division, September, 1916.

48   TNA: PRO. WO 95/360. War Diary, Third Army, September, 1916.

49   TNA: PRO. WO 95/805. War Diary, VII Corps, September, 1916.

50   Brigadier-General William James Theodore Glasgow had been the Lieutenant-Colonel of the 7th Queens, Royal West Sussex and had gone out to the Western Front in July 1915. He took over the 50th Brigade in March 1916. He was Mentioned in Despatches on 1 January 1916 and 1 January 1917.

51   Trotter had come out to the Western Front as a major in the Grenadier Guards on 19 November 1914. Promoted to Brigadier-General, he took over the 51st Brigade on 6 July 1916.

prepare plans for their two brigades to attack as ordered by VII Corps. Brigadier-General Clarke's 52nd Brigade would be the reserve. Major-General Robertson submitted his plans for the attack on 14 September and he was concerned about what the 2nd Division on his right was going to do, fearing that his men might attack with a flank in the air. Also, the vast number of guns and munitions available to the British was causing a few headaches; Major-General Robertson was worried about overcrowding. He said to General Snow,

In view of the uncertainty of the position which will obtain on this flank I am not able at present to arrange any form of co-operation with the 2nd Division ... I forwarded a tracing giving the additional ground on the south flank which I consider it imperative that I should be allowed to make use of so as to avoid crowding troops in Hébuterne. This extra area is more than necessary owing to the number of heavy batteries that are being brought into action ... [52]

Furthermore, he requested that the village of Sailly and two nearby valleys be allotted to his division for forming up and to get his men away from the British heavy batteries. When they fired it was certain that the German guns would reply with counter-battery fire endangering troop formations nearby.[53]

Set up on the high ground behind Hébuterne the big guns took their turn in wire cutting operations, targeting and destroying the big coils of defensive wire. A major operation seemed inevitable and Captain Mozley wrote that the advance "had been planned to follow up a decisive thrust by the tanks."[54] Although it seemed that he would miss it because, on 16 September, he was sent on a course at the Third Army School at Aux le Château. He noted that just before he left Blitz "told me, rather unfeelingly, that he expected the battalion would go into the attack in a few days, and that I should probably find myself

---

[52] Major-General Robertson in TNA: PRO. WO 95/1981. War Diary, 17th Division, September, 1916.

[53] TNA: PRO. WO 95/1981. War Diary, 17th Division, September, 1916.

[54] IWM: Mozley, 01/48/1.

commanding it, when I came back from the course."[55] The holiday mood had evaporated and the enemy troops and batteries on the other side of the line, once so joyfully dismissed, had taken on their former menacing proportions. Captain Mozley took Blitz's words seriously and tried to dodge the course but to no avail; run down and suffering from a crop of boils it was obvious that Captain Mozley needed a rest.[56] Meanwhile the conferences and planning meetings went on.

Simply, the 17th Division's plans were for four attacking waves to assault the first objective. The first and third waves would push on through the first German line to the second and the second and fourth waves would stop on the first line. The artillery was divided into three groups, trench mortars were to assist with wire cutting and the Stokes Mortar teams were tasked with bombarding the German communication trenches. Barrage fire was arranged. Bombers were ordered to tackle dugouts and machine gun teams were instructed to fire into gaps in the line. Pioneers and Engineers would follow the fourth wave. Digging communication trenches from the British line to connect with the captured German ones was vital and speed was of the essence, therefore Major-General Robertson asked if Corps could send an 'expert' up to reconnoitre the front line to see if 'Push Tubes'[57] could be deployed.[58] In the meantime the divisional staff worked out which British trench should be connected to which captured German trench. Provision was made for ammunition supply, water, rations, hand grenades, rifle grenades, signalling, codes were updated, sites for dumps were designated and tools were requested. In short, a good deal of work was put into the planning and preparing for the attack. Then the wire cutting operations were suspended and on 18

---

55   IWM: Mozley, 01/48/1.
56   IWM: Mozley, 01/48/1.
57   These were tubes of high explosive pushed through the ground by the 'Bartlett Forcing Jack' and once in place they were detonated. The result being a speedily excavated rough, straight trench; when they worked that is.
58   TNA: PRO. WO 95/1981. War Diary, 17th Division, September, 1916.

September the 17th Division was ordered out of the line to begin intensive training for the coming attack.[59] The attack had been postponed and there is no reason for this recorded in the VII Corps war diary, 17th Division diary or any of the brigade diaries. The reason could perhaps be found in the operations further south, not in the least the attack on the Flers – Courcelette line where the tanks made their debut on the world stage. Despite the deployment of this radical new weapon the much need deep breakthrough on the Somme did not come.

On 23 September, Captain A. P. Kennedy R.A.M.C. (Special Reserve)[60] joined Lieutenant-Colonel T. Kay's[61] 53rd Field Ambulance while they rested at Mazicourt.[62] And while the men of the 17th Division marched to a training area near Doullens, General Joffre wrote to Sir Douglas Haig. He emphasised the need for a combined effort between the French and the British, employing maximum forces to take the Bertincourt – Bapaume – Achiet le Grand line as soon as possible.[63] Sir Douglas Haig travelled by car to visit General Allenby at his Third Army H.Q., on 24 September. Sir Douglas told General Allenby to prepare an attack upon Gommecourt. His objectives were to capture and hold the village and the ridge that ran to the south-east in order to cover the left flank of General Gough's Reserve Army which would attack eastwards. General Allenby was to employ three or four divisions in his attack and between twelve to

---

59   TNA: PRO. WO 95/805. War Diary, VII Corps, September, 1916. & TNA: PRO. WO 95/1981. War Diary, 17th Division, September, 1916.

60   Kennedy arrived on the Western Front as a captain in the R.A.M.C., Special Reserve on 20 August 1914.

61   Regular army medical officer Doctor Kay first arrived on the Western Front as a lieutenant on 26 August 1914. He was soon promoted and was Mentioned in Despatches as a major on 1 January 1916. He was promoted to Lieutenant-Colonel and Mentioned in Despatches again on 9 May 1917 and 21 December 1917. He had been promoted to full Colonel by the war's end.

62   TNA: PRO. WO 95/1996. War Diary, 53rd Field Ambulance, September 1916. He was wrongly recorded as Captain P. J. Kennedy in the unit war diary.

63   J. E. Edmonds and W. Miles, *Official History Of The Great War, Military Operations France and Belgium, 1916, Vol II*, (First published, 1938. Re-printed by the Imperial War Museum and the Battery Press, 1992), p. 392

twenty-five tanks.[64] Sir Douglas had high hopes and, delighted with their performance on 15 September, wished to deploy more tanks. He wrote in his diary that day, "My intention is (if the attack comes off) to make it by surprise with a line of 50 to 60 tanks and no artillery bombardment."[65]

On 24 September there was some concern among the medical staff about the quality, health and physical state of some of the men in the 17th Division. Therefore, Colonel Oliver Richard Archer Julian,[66] the Assistant Director Medical Staff, and as such the senior medical officer in the division, had "arrangements made with 'Q'[67] Branch for inspection of men who were not up to usual physical standard or who had chronic disabilities."[68] Two days later Colonel Julian had a meeting with Lieutenant-Colonel Robert John Collins,[69] the divisional G.S.O. (1), and Lieutenant-Colonel Octavius Henry Lothian Nicholson,[70] the

---

[64] G. Sheffield & J. Bourne, (Eds), *Douglas Haig War Diaries and Letters 1914 – 1918*, (BCA, 2005), p. 233

[65] Sir Douglas Haig in Sheffield & Bourne, *Douglas Haig War Diaries and Letters 1914 – 1918*, p. 233

[66] Colonel Julian, C.M.G., had come out to the Western Front with the 17th Division on 14 July 1915. Mentioned in Despatches 1 January 1916 and 15 June 1916. He was later promoted to Major-General and awarded the C.B. and C.B.E. In 1919 he was serving in Iraq where he was awarded the General Service Medal with clasp. Julian is wrongly, initially, recorded in the 17th Division's history as 'A.D. Julian', on the second and last time he is mentioned, his proper initials are used.

[67] Adjutant and Quartermaster Branch.

[68] TNA: PRO. WO 95/1989. War Diary, A.D.M.S., September 1916.

[69] Collins of the Royal Berkshires came out to the Western Front on 27 October 1914 as a G.S.O (3) in 1 Corps, First Army. He was later promoted to Brigadier-General and took command of the 73rd Brigade, after the war he was at the Staff College, Camberley.

[70] Nicholson D.S.O., of the West Yorks had arrived on the Western Front with the B.E.F on 9 August 1914. He was a captain, a regular soldier and a specialist quartermaster. Nicholson initially served as the Military Landing Officer at Staff H.Q. No. 1 Base. Promoted to Major in 1915 he served on the 51st Brigade Staff and then moved up to become the A. A. & Q. M. G. for 17th Division with the rank of Lieutenant-Colonel. He dropped the name Octavius and always signed himself 'H. N. Nicholson' in the 17th Divisional Quartermaster's war diary. By late 1917 he was serving on the 1st Army Staff. Mentioned in Despatches 4 December 1914, 9 December 1914, 22 June 1915 and 15 May 1917. By the war's end he had been awarded the C.M.G. After the war he was on the General Staff at the War Office.

divisional Assistant Adjutant and Quartermaster General, about the coming winter and the prevention of Trench Foot and Frostbite across the division. A series of lectures had been planned by divisional H.Q for the training period so these officers decided that a number of lectures by medical officers on the subject of Trench Foot should be included in that programme.[71]

Once the 17th Division was in the rest/training area the units began to settle down to the training routine. The series of evening lectures by specialists and staff officers were arranged and the brigades were ordered to find a hall, school room or barn suitable for a lecture theatre; preferably with lighting. Major J. Fleming R.E. was to give a lecture about the responsibilities of the infantry and the engineers when consolidating positions. G.S.O (1), Lieutenant-Colonel Collins was to lecture about inter communications, information and reporting. An artillery officer was to talk about the capabilities of the guns and howitzers and co-operation between the infantry and gunners. Major Barnett was down to give a lecture about Returns, Courts Martial and Administration and, of course, there would be the lectures about Trench Foot. Further lectures were to be announced and full lecture notes would be available so that officers could return to their units and pass the information on to their colleagues.[72] These notes would doubtless be useful as well to those officers who dozed off during the lectures because everyone was busy morning, noon and night.

The 9th Duke of Wellingtons' diary tell us that training at this time was intense. The hours of work were 8 am to Noon, 2 pm to 4 pm with the lectures running from 5.30 pm to 6.30 pm. Major Campbell gave a memorable lecture, with demonstrations on the art of bayonet fighting. The C.Os, 2 i/cs, adjutants and assistant adjutants were lectured about correspondence and returns. Lectures were given on the limitations and uses of tanks

---

71 TNA: PRO. WO 95/1989. War Diary, A.D.M.S., September 1916.
72 TNA: PRO. WO 95/1981. War Diary, 17th Division, September, 1916.

and the men were given demonstrations of the tanks in action and on the practical side the battalions trained to take and consolidate trenches and how to co-operate with a creeping barrage. Communications with aircraft were practiced and men regularly took part in physical exercise and close order drill. A large number of this particular battalion attended Church Parades. When the working day was done passes were issued to men of good character. Their C.O., Major Simner kept the men of his battalion on their toes and made it one of the best battalions in the 52nd Brigade and the 17th Division.[73]

Across the division officers undertook training without their companies or platoons and then with them. The officers and men were put through regular physical training and close order drill. Marching by night to given locations and marching by compass bearing was practiced at company level. Then surprise locations, with compass bearings were given to companies as they were on the march in the dark and they had to find their way to the new destinations. Map reading lessons were given. Practice was given to moving working parties laden with tools to locations at speed and in co-operation with the Royal Engineers the infantry learned how to consolidate captured positions and set up battle out-posts. They saw the trench digging explosive tubes in action. Companies were trained to move under artillery fire and attention was given to reconnaissance training, patrolling and reporting. Specialists honed their arts. The artillery practiced moving swiftly into action, gun battery drills and visual communications were carried out and importantly the men were given demonstrations of the new tank. In short, they were training for open, break-through warfare.

Sir Douglas was keen to keep up the pressure on the German Army, believing the intelligence that told him, on the Somme, the German Army was at breaking point. However, there were

---

[73] TNA: PRO. WO 95/2014. War Diary, 9th Duke of Wellingtons, West Riding Regiment, September 1916.

signs that some in the French High command were considering closing down operations for the winter. Sir Douglas wrote in his diary on 28 September, "General Foch came to see me at 2.30 pm ... He is prepared to continue the battle into November or until the bad weather stops all chance of attacking."[74] Unlike General Foch, who was probably aware of what a severe winter in Picardy could be like, Sir Douglas was keen to pursue the campaign throughout the winter without a pause.

On the following day, 29 September, Sir Douglas ordered that the Reserve,[75] Third and Fourth Armies should combine their actions and they were instructed to make preparations for a large scale attack.[76] The Armies were given their objectives. General Allenby's Third Army was to take Gommecourt. General Rawlinson's Fourth Army, down south on the Somme, which joined with the French forces on its right flank, was tasked with taking "Le Transloy, Beaulencourt, ridge beyond the Thilloy – Warlencourt Valley, Loupart Wood (1 mile E. of Irles)."[77] This would suggest that there had been a pause but that was not the case, along the line the fighting and shelling continued. In a discussion with General Rawlinson, Sir Douglas told him that when Le Transloy was captured arrangements should at once be made to push onto Beaulencourt in co-operation with the French.[78] General Rawlinson had no objections to attacking Le Transloy. His Fourth Army was lying in the bottom of a valley, a bad place to be in terms of things rolling down hill and even worse because the German observers could look down on the

---

[74] Sheffield & Bourne, *Douglas Haig War Diaries and Letters 1914 – 1918*, p. 235
[75] Soon to become Fifth Army.
[76] Miles, *Official History, 1916*, Vol II, p. 427
[77] Miles, *Official History, 1916*, Vol II, p. 427
[78] R. Prior & T. Wilson, *Command on the Western Front, The Military Career of Sir Henry Rawlinson 1914 – 1918*, (Blackwell Publishers, 1992. Re-printed, Pen & Sword, 2004), p. 256

British and see much of what they did.[79] To get out of the low valley and up onto the ridge was desirable and sensible.

On 1 October the B.E.F. put all clocks and watches back one hour to Winter Time[80] and after completing their training the 17th Division returned to the Third Army's Gommecourt sector to find the place buzzing in preparation for the coming offensive. Lieutenant Hoyte wrote,

> *On arrival at Baynecourt on October 2nd we found arrangements going forward at the very highest pressure for a great advance on the Gommecourt front. Howitzer batteries sprang up like mushrooms in the night around Sailly au Bois; enormous dumps of bombs, S.A.A., Very Lights etc. were made in the trenches and carrying parties were incessant for the formation of these dumps. The artillery started cutting wire on the enemy front, and tank tracks were made. Pages and pages of instructions were vomited forth by Brigade H.Q., all for Zero Day.[81]*

On his return to the 6th Dorsets Captain Mozley found that his men were busy still practising on dummy trenches.[82] On 3 October, Rifleman Harry Poole of the 7th Yorks deserted.

In his report of 7 October 1916 Sir Douglas still foresaw no break in operations, he knew that his men had made gains and was determined that their progress and sacrifice should be followed up. On the Somme front the Germans troops had pulled back to less formidable positions than the ones already won from them over the summer. Added to this the German Army had lost an estimated 370,000 men, killed and wounded, on the Somme up to October 1916.[83] Although the bad weather was taking hold Sir Douglas can be forgiven for believing that

79 Fourth Army papers, Vol VI, Conference at Heilly, 18 October 1916 in Prior & Wilson, *Command on the Western Front, The Military Career of Sir Henry Rawlinson 1914 – 1918*, p. 255

80 TNA: PRO. WO 95/2014. War Diary, 9th Duke of Wellingtons, West Riding Regiment, October 1916.

81 Hoyte, *10th (S) Battalion*, p. 21

82 IWM: Mozley, 01/48/1.

83 Miles, *Official History, 1916*, Vol II, p. 456

more applied pressure would give his armies a major breakthrough and that a normal winter would not hamper their operations. British casualties had been high and an enormous amount of war munitions[84] had been expended. Therefore what concerned him was the replenishment of men and materials, better communications and improved accommodation for the coming winter to allow operations to continue.[85] As the Official History says,

In conclusion, Sir Douglas Haig urged that the "utmost efforts of the Empire" should be directed towards enabling him to continue the offensive without intermission: It was not possible to say how near to breaking point the enemy might be, but there was fair prospect of a far-reaching success "affording full compensation for all that has been done to attain it": any relaxation of effort would, on the contrary, discount the great advantages already gained.[86]

In the 'Chief's' mind there was no alternative but to continue to put pressure on the Western Front, even if the Somme had not been his choice of battlefield,[87] because it was where the enemy was; occupying the land of an allied nation. His personal Chaplain, temporary 4th Class, the Reverend, G. S. Duncan,[88] a man intimately acquainted with Sir Douglas' mind wrote,

---

[84] This is the Great War term for all things used by the military; from shells to buttons and bullets to boxes.

[85] Miles, *Official History, 1916*, Vol II, p. 456

[86] Miles, *Official History, 1916*, Vol II, p. 456 - 457

[87] It was General Joffre's choice.

[88] Sir Douglas Haig heard the young Reverend Duncan give a simple Presbyterian service in St. Omer and returned every Sunday thereafter. When Sir Douglas moved his H.Q. to Montreuil he took the Chaplain with him. Duncan was Mentioned in Despatches on 17 January 1917. The two men remained friends until Sir Douglas' death in 1928. Duncan felt compelled, late in life, to write a short book about his observations of the 'Chief' because of the distorted and largely false image of the Field Marshal that was growing up in popular culture in the 1960s. Duncan had felt that his relationship with Haig had been too personal to publish but he was ultimately moved to speak out for his friend. Dr Duncan, Moderator of the General Assembly of the Church of Scotland, died the year

In a war of this magnitude, in which Britain was being called to bear an ever-increasing burden, Haig knew that casualties were bound to be heavy. If, with Mr. Lloyd George, he could have persuaded himself that victory could be achieved in some circuitous and less costly way, how gladly would he have welcomed it. But as a realist he was convinced that there was no such way... [89]

So, Sir Douglas was intent on pushing forward but as the Official History continued, "His hopes of carrying out the extensive operations planned for the end of September were fading, [90] although he intended to attempt all that the weather conditions allowed; and he had already settled upon the reorganization of his forces with a view to maintaining the utmost pressure upon the enemy throughout the winter." [91] As mentioned, Sir Douglas firmly believed that the Germans were near to breaking point, all of the intelligence gathered by General Rawlinson's Fourth Army indicated that fact. By mid to late September the German First Army held the line from Le Transloy to the River Ancre with six divisions, all weakened by the heavy fighting. Units and battalions from other divisions had been fed into the battle in an ad hoc manner and those six divisions were not only weak but mixed up. Added to this the German positions were defensively poor with few dugouts and little wire. [92]

Up at Gommecourt orders and tables for the attack were distributed throughout the 17th Division on 11 October. On 16 October the plans for the attack on Gommecourt were still active and there was no reason to doubt that the offensive would soon go ahead. On the following day the 50th Brigade took over

---

before his book was published. (Information from the flyleaf of *Douglas Haig As I Knew Him*).

[89] G. S. Duncan, *Douglas Haig As I Knew Him,* (George Allen and Unwin Ltd, First published, 1966), p. 48

[90] Miles, *Official History, 1916*, Vol II, p. 427

[91] Miles, *Official History, 1916*, Vol II, p. 457

[92] Fourth Army Intelligence Summaries 20 August – 16 November, 1916. In Prior & Wilson, *Command on the Western Front, The Military Career of Sir Henry Rawlinson 1914 – 1918*, p. 252

a section of the front line from the 19th Brigade but soon orders arrived for them to be relieved in the line once more.

By 18 October, even as the artillery continued with their wire cutting operations for the offensive, orders were issued then a few hours later countermanded. Lieutenant-Colonel Fife, who was ill again and with some justification irritable and grumpy, wrote an entry that while expressing frustration sheds some light on the plans for the planned Gommecourt Offensive and an infantry officer's views on that planned attack. The entry also highlighted the lack of up to date movement information at battalion level.

At 2.30 pm orders for relief tomorrow arrived. At 4 pm orders for relief tonight arrived. The first order was that on relief tomorrow we were to march to Hénu but this destination has been changed to Sailly, which we left yesterday. I wish the Higher Command could make up their minds and stick to their plans. Relief not completed until 8 pm by which time a cold, which began yesterday, had made me almost speechless … It seems as though the attack on the Gommecourt Salient has been abandoned. On the map the scheme possesses obvious advantages as a successful advance to Bucquoy and Achiet le Grand, combined with the capture of Bapaume from the south would result in the loss of all German positions southwards of the Ancre and a large haul of prisoners, but the Gommecourt position is enormously strong and after studying the ground most carefully I don't think the attack would succeed. An attack north of Gommecourt, to Essarts, would appear more promising …[93]

On 19 October the division was relieved in the line and began to journey south. [94] To some, Lieutenant-Colonel Fife included, there was surprise and an amount of uncertainty as to what was going on and where they were going. The notion that the division would be sent south to the Somme did not seem to have

93 Personal Diary of Lieutenant-Colonel Fife.
94 TNA: PRO. WO 95/1981. War Diary, 17th Division, October, 1916.

entered Lieutenant-Colonel Fife's head. He wrote in his diary on that day,

> *A cold wet morning. Marched at 12.30 for Halloy, arriving there at 5 pm. The marching of the men has much improved. Received orders for all transport to leave us shortly, the battalion to be conveyed "south" by motor bus on 21ˢᵗ. I don't know why they say south unless they mean north.*[95]

But they were not going north; the offensive at Gommecourt was off. G.H.Q. had changed the plans and the 17ᵗʰ Division, forced to abandon all of the plans and preparations for the Third Army attack,[96] was ordered south to the Somme to join General Frederick Rudolph Lambart, the Earl Cavan's XIV Corps which was in the line facing Le Transloy.[97]

Operations at Le Transloy, in strategic terms, were to provide a new start point for the resumption of major operations in the New Year. In tactical terms it was to establish a new front line on the crest of the ridge in front of Le Transloy, allowing depth in defence and providing a good jumping off point for an attack should the opportunity arise at any given moment. In simple terms it was to capture German front line positions, move the British/French front line forward and get out of the valley.

On the German side matters had changed considerably since the Fourth Army intelligence officers analysed the German First Army in September and gave Sir Douglas cause for optimism. The worn out divisions on the Le Transloy – Ancre line were replaced by seven fresh ones between 30 September and 13 October. In addition, twenty-three new artillery batteries had been added to the German gun line and thirty-six exhausted and

---

[95] Personal Diary of Lieutenant-Colonel Fife.

[96] There is a post script to this however. The training that the 17ᵗʰ Division did while it was with the Third Army up at Gommecourt in 1916 was not forgotten. It is more than likely one of the major reasons that Third Army chose the division to work with the Cavalry for rapid deployment in open warfare in the plans for the Battle of Arras in 1917.

[97] TNA: PRO. WO 95/1981. War Diary, 17ᵗʰ Division, October 1916.

worn out batteries had been withdrawn.[98] First Army had also learned how to counter the British creeping barrage that in September had so effectively destroyed the machine gun posts set up between the trench lines. The machine guns were withdrawn to the extremity of their range from where they could still inflict casualties on the British but were beyond the creeping barrage. It was intelligence that the British appear to have missed and a change of tactic that the British failed to identify in October.[99] The weather was closing in as well as heavy rain fell and the temperature began to drop.

Reinforcements were needed for the new push by Fourth Army at Le Transloy, therefore the 17th Division had been recalled to the Somme front as part of the restructuring of the Armies. The 17th Division was officially transferred from Third Army, VII Corps to Fourth Army, XIV Corps on 21 October.[100] On 27 October the troops of the 17th Division began to arrive on the Somme.[101]

---

[98] Der Weltkrieg, Vol II, p. 80 – 1. In Prior & Wilson, *Command on the Western Front, The Military Career of Sir Henry Rawlinson 1914 – 1918*, p. 252

[99] Prior & Wilson, *Command on the Western Front, The Military Career of Sir Henry Rawlinson 1914 – 1918*, p. 253

[100] TNA: PRO. WO 95/1981. War Diary, 17th Division, October 1916.

[101] TNA: PRO. WO 95/1981. War Diary, 17th Division, October 1916.

The Camps and The Line

Camps

Heavy rain was punctuated by hail showers on 27 October and it was bitterly cold as the battalions marched along the wrecked, mud-paste roads, where German prisoners and British troops toiled together in a fruitless battle to repair them. Captain Mozley, A Company, 6th Dorsets, wrote, "The roads were ghastly. They were originally only country roads and had been put into an awful state by shelling, rain, mud, heavy transport, guns and anything else that was likely to contribute towards their destruction." [102]

Such was the appalling state of the roads and tracks into and across this part of the Somme battlefield a huge amount of labour was required to just attempt to mend them, sometimes whole battalions of infantry were called upon. The 7th Borders, 51st Brigade, noted in their War Diary that on 28 October, the day after arriving at the Citadel, "whole battalion on working party repairing the Montauban – Peronne Road under the C. E. XIV Corps."[103] The 10th West Yorks, 50th Brigade, arrived on the Somme on 27 October and they took over A Camp, Mansel Camp, near Mametz from the 1st Royal Dublin Fusiliers. On 28 October they were employed making chalk pathways to and from the front line.[104]

---

[102] IWM: Mozley, 01/48/1.
[103] TNA: PRO. WO 95/2008. War Diary, 7th Borders, October 1916.
[104] TNA: PRO. WO 95/2004. War Diary, 10th West Yorks, October 1916.

As they arrived on the Somme the battalions were sent to different camps in their brigade areas, for instance, Sandpits Camp at Meaulte, the Citadel near Fricourt and Mansell Camp at Mansell Copse near Mametz Village. Other camps did not even have names and so were reduced to letters or numbers, for instance F Camp and H Camp among others and T8 Central was named from its map reference.[105] Bernafay Wood was an important camp complex and once properly organised it became the site of a number of headquarters. The camps did not provide a pleasant experience, given the conditions, and none of the camps was better than any other. In theory the battalions should have travelled smoothly from one camp to another as they moved to and from the front line. As usual things did not always go to plan; wrecked, inadequate, congested and frequently shelled roads in this part of rural France slowed movement down to a snail's pace and the weather always played a part in slowing things down even further. Orders, issued by the multitude of chains of command could always confuse matters and the camps were frequently occupied by more than one formation and were overcrowded.

Getting into the camps could be a tricky matter. Captain Mozley wrote, "We made an early move, leaving Meaulte at 7.30 a.m., and arriving at a camp near Mansell Copse at about 9 a.m. The outgoing battalion had not yet moved, so we had to wait for two hours on a bleak hillside."[106] Lieutenant-Colonel Ronald D'Arcy Fife,[107] C.O., of the 7th Yorks, the Green Howards, 50th Brigade, wrote of a similar experience,

---

105 T 8 Central later became a large munitions dump.

106 IWM: Mozley, 01/48/1.

107 He had been in command of his battalion since its formation in Richmond in 1914. He was wounded by a 5.9-inch shell on 13 February 1917 and deafened. His wounds took years to heal and he remained deaf for the rest of his life. He never returned to his unit or to the fighting. Fife did, however, join the Home Guard in WW II as a private soldier. His CO was his own gamekeeper. From the Personal diary of Lieutenant-Colonel Fife held at the Green Howards museum, Richmond.

Got up at 4 and breakfasted at 5 in order that mess kit might be loaded. Marched at 7 to new camp and arrived there at 8. To find that the Battalion in occupation were not under orders to move till 11. The Battalion therefore waited on a very exposed hill side in a cold wind and rain for 3 hours.[108]

Once they got into a camp, their troubles were far from over. Unless one was with divisional H.Q., (efforts were made to billet H.Qs in huts)[109] dry accommodation did not exist, although there were sometimes dugouts and covered trenches and the odd hut, the best that could be hoped for was an already soaked, leaking, Bell Tent with no ground sheet. Lower down the accommodation ladder were shell holes and old gun pits covered by leaking tarpaulins and at the bottom was a hole in the ground, open to the elements. Lieutenant Colonel Fife noted sourly, "The camp, when we reached it, was not luxurious, being very muddy. The men were close packed. 17 in each bell tent. Very heavy rain in the evening."[110] Captain Mozley reinforced Fife's diary entry, "Very few tents were available, and the men were rather squashed."[111] Major Frederick Blaine, the C.O., of D Company, 7th York & Lancaster Pioneers, was with his men at F Camp near Montauban, until the previous day D Company had been billeted at Ville-sur-Ancre. Blaine was unimpressed with F Camp because they were housed in sodden tents, "that stood

---

108 Personal diary of Lieutenant-Colonel Fife.

109 This was not a case of making sure that the General and his staff were warm and dry at the expense of the 'poor bloody infantry'. The division was the administrative heart of the fighting formations that made up the brigades. If the administration failed then the division would fail to function and at the core of the organisation was paperwork and there was tons of it. That paperwork had to remain dry. Administration has all too often been ignored and when it has been mentioned it has often been to denigrate the service for being in the rear. If a division or brigade does not have administrative organisation and good logistics then the battalions and companies have problems in the field.

110 Personal diary of Lieutenant-Colonel Fife.

111 IWM: Mozley, 01/48/1.

out cheerless and uninviting, like spectres in a wilderness of ruin, desolation and mud."[112]

No one wanted to live under these conditions and the following day the officers ordered their men to construct proper camps. Not only would such activity improve their lot, it would warm them up, get their circulation going and in taking their minds off grousing, it would improve their morale. With violent artillery bombardments providing a backdrop the men set to work. Lieutenant-Colonel Fife said, "Whole Battalion employed in improving camp, which is in a most filthy state."[113] They worked with a will and Captain Mozley wrote, "Messes and cookhouses were built, and we felt that we should shake down quite comfortably…"[114] Latrines and even wash stands were fabricated. If items and materials were left lying around or unattended then they were 'lifted' in the blink of an eye, anything that would improve the soldiers' lot was taken. Captain Sidney Rogerson, 2nd West Yorks, who served in this sector at the same time, wrote of such an incident in his book *Twelve Days On The Somme.*

"I congratulate you on your servant," the Colonel said casually. "Why sir?" I queried. "Well, as I walked into the very commodious trench shelter reserved for Battalion Headquarters, I saw your man walking out at the other end with the stove. And you hadn't been in camp five minutes! A good boy that. But I'm sorry I could not spare the stove!" The Colonel smiled and moved on.[115]

Being resourceful the Tommies scavenged and scrounged whatever material that they could, and a stove was a highly prized piece of booty. Trench systems and dugouts were a rich source of wood and considered fair game to the marauding

112 Major Blaine in M. Gilvary, *History Of The 7th Service Battalion The York And Lancaster Regiment (Pioneers) 1914 -1919.* (The Talbot Press, Ltd, 1921) p. 27

113 Personal diary of Lieutenant-Colonel Fife.

114 IWM: Mozley, 01/48/1.

115 S. Rogerson, *Twelve Days On The Somme, A Memoir of the Trenches, 1916*, (First published 1933, Re-published, Greenhill Books, 2006), p.15

soldiers.[116] Unfortunately the removal of timbers made the dugouts even more unsafe than they initially were and the wet weather made such temporary ground based structures dangerous for the unwary. Privates three, Hall, Middlehurst and Trusswell of the 52nd Brigade Machine Gun Company took up residence in an empty dugout at D Camp in Bernafay Wood. It promptly collapsed and buried them;[117] a mixed group of Australians and Northumberland Fusiliers who were billeted nearby set to and dug them out.[118]

In some cases the men's work on their camps was in vain because they were moved on to another camp, leaving their efforts half-finished or finished and available for the next incoming battalion. The 10th Yorks cleaned up A Camp at Mansel Camp on 27 and 28 October, in between making chalk paths, but they were moved forward on 29 October and marched to another A Camp that lay between Bernafay and Trones Woods. They had a day of rest there before going into the line, to relieve the 2nd West Yorks of the 8th Division, north of Les Boeufs.[119]

For some the camps were overcrowded and it was the story of 'no room at the Inn' as the 29th Mobile Veterinary Section discovered. On 31 October they were sent to Minden Post and the journey there was dire, "Owing to the congested state of the roads, 4 hours was taken to do a distance of 1 kilometre. OC decided to make use of tracks across country."[120] When they arrived it was discovered that the camp, as usual, was in a dreadful state. "The camp was very muddy and totally unsuitable for the reception of sick animals though very

---

[116] TNA: PRO. WO 95/2002. War Diary, 7th East Yorks, October 1916.

[117] Hall, Middlehurst and Trusswell were none the worse for their experience and all survived the war.

[118] TNA: PRO. WO 95/2014. War Diary, 52nd Brigade Machine Gun Company, October 1916.

[119] TNA: PRO. WO 95/2004. War Diary, 10th West Yorks, October 1916.

[120] TNA: PRO. WO 95/1997. War Diary, 29th Mobile Veterinary Section, October 1916.

convenient to rail head, a distance of 200 yards."[121] Their colleagues from the 8th Division's Mobile Veterinary Section were still there and had no orders to move.

As usual accommodation was an issue, this time for animals as well as humans, and on the following morning after cramming in together wherever they could find shelter it was decided to move their camp, "nearer to the road owing to long muddy approach to horse lines. Space taken over being small & confined."[122] Despite this they were still unhappy with their position and sought a drier camp that could accommodate the sick animals. They tried Carnoy where they had heard there were dugouts but the camp was overrun by infantry and there was no room for them. Moving on again the Section arrived at Mansell Copse, near Mansell Camp, here using a few tents successfully scrounged (or 'won') from the infantry at the camp, about six days after arriving back on the Somme, the Vets set up a camp where they could house and treat animals. It just about suited their needs in terms of space for sick animals and it was a reasonable distance to the rail head from where the animals could be evacuated. They were also in a favourite target area for the German artillery because the railway always attracted the attention of the gunners. All of the time that they had been peripatetic they had been trying to care for the sick animals that were constantly brought to them. Sometimes they treated civilians' animals as well. [123]

The signallers had a similar story, work began just as soon as they arrived in the sector. The 17th Division's H.Q. opened at Minden Post on 31 October and a divisional reporting centre to handle communication with the three brigades was established at Bernafay Wood. Here the 220 officers and men of the 17th

---

121 TNA: PRO. WO 95/1997. War Diary, 29th Mobile Veterinary Section, October 1916.
122 TNA: PRO. WO 95/1997. War Diary, 29th Mobile Veterinary Section, October & November, 1916.
123 TNA: PRO. WO 95/1997. War Diary, 29th Mobile Veterinary Section, October – November, 1916.

Divisional Signals Company set to work on the existing cables. Communication to the brigades they noted was erratic because of the poor state of the cables, therefore Linesmen went straight out to deal with them and were soon mending breaks in the 'air lines'[124] or ground cables. It was a constant endeavour; air raids, shelling and accidents destroyed or damaged the cables and communication by telephone was often lost to Corps and the brigades so whatever the time, conditions or situation the Linesmen had to go out and solve the problems. Nonetheless, their work and commitment paid off because on average the brigades were in telephone communication with the battalions for fourteen hours a day. On the other hand the battalions were out of communication with the brigades for ten hours a day. In November the Company lost only two men killed and seven wounded.[125] It might sound callous but considering the shelling and air raids these were good figures.

There was no grousing about conditions or the camps from the 51st, 52nd or 53rd Field Ambulances, they simply arrived and got on with their work. The 53rd Field Ambulance arrived in the area earlier than the other units because it was tasked with taking over the XIV Corps Rest Station at Dive Copse between Morlancourt, Sailly-le-Sec and Sailly-Laurette. The Station had been a dressing station but appears to have changed its function at the end of September. The 53rd Field Ambulance took over on 23 October and was to remain there until late January 1917. The Rest Station comprised a series of large tents that housed patients, medical personnel, drivers, vehicles, animals and stores. It appears to have handled largely sickness cases and if patients could not be treated and returned to their units they were evacuated to base hospitals. Such was the size and intake of the Station, detachments from other Field Ambulances, such as the 3rd, 80th and 101st, were at times temporarily posted to Dive

---

124 Suspended telegraph and telephone wires.
125 TNA: PRO. WO 95/1994. War Diary, 17th Signal Company, October – November, 1916.

Copse to assist. From 23 October through to 14 November when the 17th Division was pulled out of the line the medics at Dive Copse received 6,553 officers and men. Of these patients 3,584 were evacuated to base hospitals and 2,104 were returned to duty with their units.[126] This left a difference of 865 patients who presumably remained on the wards during this time. Only one patient was recorded as having died and that was on 30 October.[127]

The Field Ambulances also took over the Advanced Dressing Station in Bernafay Wood and the Advanced Relay Post at Lesboeufs, the Regimental Aid Post at Gueudecourt and the Medical Relay Posts or Bearer Posts up to the front line. [128] The post at Lesboeufs was manned by one medical officer and seventeen bearers. An Advanced Dressing Station was maintained by two medical officers and twenty-one bearers and Bearer Posts were manned by one N.C.O and twelve to sixteen bearers. Casualties were carried from post to post away from the front line by relays of bearers to ambulances in the rear area. The Field Ambulances relieved each other every other day. The medical posts were not immune to shelling or air attack and the bearers and their animals were wounded and killed as they worked.[129] Private Joseph Brown, of the 51st Field Ambulance,

---

[126] TNA: PRO. WO 95/1996. War Diary, 53rd Field Ambulance, October – November 1916.

[127] The War Diary does not record any deaths bar the one on 30 October 1916. The nearest cemetery, Dive Copse, contains 589 casualties and they were in the main from July to September 1916, then some from 1918 and other bodies were brought in after the war ended. Only one man was buried there in November 1916, Private Henry James Godbold M2/032940, Army Service Corps who died 18 November 1916, presumably of sickness at the Rest Station. The cemetery was not in use from September 1916 onwards therefore, apart from isolated cases, this suggests that swathes of patients were NOT dying at the Rest Station.

[128] During the Somme Campaign the three Field Ambulances of the 17th Division used different names for medical posts and positions. There seems to have been no standardisation of titles at this time.

[129] TNA: PRO. WO 95/1996. War Diaries, 51st, 52nd and 53rd Field Ambulances, October – November 1916.

was killed by shellfire on 4 November.[130] Private S. Walter Reynolds, 52nd Field Ambulance, suffered the indignity of being shot in the buttocks and was then wounded again by a shell while he was at No. 3 Bearer Post,[131] presumably while being treated. Reynolds survived his injuries and the war.

Work

All around the Somme battlefield lay detritus and the evidence of savage fighting. Lieutenant-Colonel Fife wrote in his diary about a walk he and one of his officers went on,

> ... *through Delville Wood and Longeuval. Both are the most hideous wastes imaginable. A great many unburied Boche corpses are lying about, with many loose arms and legs. There are not ten yards anywhere without a shell hole ... East of Delville Wood I saw more dead Boches than I have seen anywhere. Two tanks are lying stranded in the mud. Some artillery officers are living in one of them.*[132]

This devastated area had recently been successive front lines and no-man's-land as the Fourth Army slowly advanced, therefore there was plenty of construction work to do to make it habitable and more accessible. Engineers and Pioneers were in great demand and as such were stretched to the limit. Therefore, as usual, the infantry were expected to provide labour for the huge number of jobs of work that came up.

The companies of the 7th Yorks & Lancs, Pioneers, whose H.Q. was at the Citadel, were on detached duty across the area. They were under the direct control of the 17th Division and were employed maintaining forward communications, roads and

---

130 TNA: PRO. WO 95/1996. War Diaries, 51st Field Ambulance, October – November 1916.
131 TNA: PRO. WO 95/1996. War Diaries, 52nd Field Ambulance, October – November 1916.
132 Personal diary of Lieutenant-Colonel Fife.

trenches. Some of the battalion were employed at Bernafay Wood Camp constructing the new Divisional Headquarters complex. Bernafay Wood was the regular haunt of the young Prince of Wales and the fact that he was present was not missed even by the Other Ranks. Stretcher Bearer Corporal Harlow, 10th Notts & Derbys, recalled that, "the Prince of Wales was on the staff of this [XIV] Corps."[133] It is no secret that the Prince wanted to get into the fighting but the Palace and the High Command simply would not allow it. Otherwise, Haig took a relaxed view to the Prince's involvement with the war effort; after all what else could he do about having the heir to the British throne wandering around the Western Front? Later on in the war the Prince was allowed to "join whichever Army H.Q. happens to be engaged in the most interesting operations at the time."[134] Haig wrote of him,

> *He seems a good sporting lad, natural and sincere, but rather faddy over his diet. Eats no breakfast, but has jam in large quantities with 'morning tea'. His small stature makes me think he was starved as a baby.[135]*

Prince Edward got as close to the front line as he could and while worrying his minders as he did so he earned the respect of many of the ordinary rank and file. Lieutenant Hoyte wrote,

> *The Prince of Wales was attached to the Corps Staff, and in the following months he was often seen on the duckboards in the forward area, followed by a staff officer who always looked extremely anxious both for his own and the Prince's safety.[136]*

It has been said that the Great War shaped his view of life; if that was the case he would not have been the only youngster who came out of the war a changed person. Perhaps some of

---

133 Imperial War Museum (IWM): Unpublished papers, Corporal Eric H. Harlow, M.M. 03/15/1.

134 Sheffield & Bourne, Haig, p.463

135 Sheffield & Bourne, Haig, p.474

136 Hoyte, *10th (S) Battalion*, p. 24

what he saw in and around the camps on the Somme in 1916 had some bearing on his 'devil may care' attitude to life after the war; an attitude that ultimately shocked the British establishment to its core in 1936. However, in 1916, he was another young staff officer from H.Q., haunting the forward areas.

When the 78th Field Company, R.E, arrived at their new camp near Waterlot Farm they found no shelter at all. There was just the beginnings of a camp that had just been started by their colleagues of 2nd Field Company, R.E. just before they were moved on to another place. Fortunately, the Engineers had access to tools, dugout material, timber and pontoon wagons, so the officers and men began work on the new camp straight away. They needed to get out of the rain.[137] There were a few old hands in the ranks who had been on the Somme before and cynicism was creeping in. Sapper F. Palmer Cook of the 78th Field Company was one such solider. He was unimpressed with their lot and recalled,

Our Somme Offensive began with high hopes of ending the war, it ground to a halt in October and we were back to trench warfare again and mud, with very little to show for it except a few miles of devastated country and enormous casualties. Still we were stubborn and we endured another winter consolidating a line in a hollow stretch of water-logged terrain, kindly left us by the enemy who was sitting on the Bapaume ridge with a balcony view to watch every movement we made in the depths below.[138]

While some Sappers from the 78th Field Company, R.E, took pontoon wagons from their camp at Waterlot Farm to Minden Post and Guillemont to collect more materials and stores, all other available men were employed working on their own camp. In order to prioritise the list of jobs that they had to do Captain

---

[137] TNA: PRO. WO 95/1993. War Diary, 78th Field Company, R.E., October 1916.

[138] Imperial War Museum (IWM): Unpublished papers of Sapper and later Colonel, F. Palmer Cook, O.B.E., T.D. 81/44/1.

C. F. Carson,[139] the company commander, and his officers worked out a program of work. The duckboard walkway to 50th Brigade H.Q. at T8 Central was in a very bad way and needed to be repaired. It also needed to be extended forward as soon as more duckboards could be obtained, they would have to be salvaged if no new ones could be obtained. Dugouts needed to be excavated in the trenches and their own camp at Waterlot Farm had to be completed. Captain Carson prioritised the work for the division as follows,

(1) Communications.

(2) Dugouts.

(3) General improvement of trenches, duckboards – shelters etc.[140]

It is interesting to note that work on their own camp did not even appear on the list of priorities, however, it was about to become extremely important.

By the afternoon on 1 November the sections of sappers working on their own shelters had completed their task and the 78th Field Company had somewhere dry and warm to rest. At 4.30 that afternoon orders arrived from the divisional C.R.E., saying that the 78th Field Company had to provide accommodation for the 50th Brigade staff who would be arriving from T8 Central on the following morning. Carson had no alternative but to evict his men from the new shelters that they had made for themselves in preparation for the arrival of the 50th Brigade staff.[141]

---

[139] C. F. Carson, R.E., earned a Mention in Despatches in June 1916, was promoted to Major in December 1916 and was awarded the M.C., in January 1917. He remained in the Royal Engineers and after the war served in India.

[140] TNA: PRO WO 95/1993. War Diary, 78th Field Company, R.E, October to November 1916.

[141] TNA: PRO WO 95/1993. War Diary, 78th Field Company, R.E, October to November 1916.

During the early morning the 50th Brigade arrived and were duly housed in the new shelters meant for the sappers. Then, at 10.00 am, entirely un-announced, the 51st Brigade H.Q. staff arrived expecting the 78th Field Company to house them as well. He had no orders to do so but Captain Carson had no choice, even though the vast majority of his company were out doing other jobs and at this time an R.E., Field Company would only be about 200 strong,[142] he ordered all of the men he had spare, one section, to construct bivouacs for the staff and the sappers. The work took all day and went on into the night but by 11.30 pm Carson had everyone under cover. Orders for Carson's company to construct billets for the 51st Brigade staff arrived from divisional H.Q at 11.15 pm. Construction began on the following day to provide proper, more permanent brigade H.Q. accommodation. Work continued on improving the camps, mining dugouts, draining trenches, laying and repairing duckboards and maintaining the trenches.[143] There were water pipes to lay, cable trenches to dig, cables to lay with the Signallers and the roads needed constant repair. On the Somme, in 1916, rest camps did not mean rest by any stretch of the imagination.

Despite the filthy state of the camps and the area in general there were attempts to clean things up, therefore the 34th Sanitary Section had plenty of work to do. Under the command of Captain E. R. Matthews, R.A.M.C, (T),[144] the men were spread across the area doing what their war diary recorded with grim

---

142 For instance the 93rd Field Company recorded their strength in November as six officers and 208 men; not forgetting the 74 horses. TNA: PRO. WO 95/1993. War Diary, 93rd Field Company R.E., November 1916.

143 TNA: PRO. WO 95/1993. War Diary, 78th Field Company, R.E, October to November 1916.

144 Captain Matthews always signed the war diary using the letter 'T' after R.A.M.C. It means that he was a temporary, wartime officer. Perhaps this status was something that he wanted to re-affirm every month! Indeed during October, November and December the keeper of the 53rd Field Ambulance war diary made a point of always differentiating between regular and temporary medical officers. If a doctor was a wartime officer he was always 'Tempy' or 'T' in the diary.

and daily regularity as, "Routine duties in Div. area."[145] These duties were itemised as follows,

"Routine Work" includes,

(1)   Inspection of billets occupied by troops.

(2)   Cleansing of streets.

(3)   Removal of refuse from billets and houses occupied by civilian population.

(4)   Incineration of such refuse.

(5)   Cleaning of cesspits.

(6)   Periodic testing of water from wells.

(7)   Disinfection of infected billets.

(8)   General supervision of the area occupied by the division.

(9)   Supervision of the burial of horses.

(10) Cleaning of drains.[146]

These duties had been first laid down in June 1916 and some of the items possibly did not apply on the Somme in October/November 1916. Nonetheless, the list of work shows just how busy the Sanitary Section was. [147]   To add to their load they had to organise and supervise the communal baths when possible.[148] Pioneer officer C.P. Blacker, 4th Coldstream Guards, Guards Division, who was in the area at the time, recalled that

145 TNA: PRO. WO 95/1997. War Diary, 34th Sanitary Section, October to November 1916.

146 TNA: PRO. WO 95/1997. War Diary, 34th Sanitary Section, June 1916.

147 When the division came out of the line they had ten villages under their care, Cavillon, Picquigny, Oissy, Molliens-Vidame, Camps-en-Amienois, Montagne, Ailly-sur-Somme, Breilly, Saissemont and Suasseval, and it was their duty to leave them in a better sanitary state then when they arrived.

148 TNA: PRO. WO 95/1997. War Diary, 34th Sanitary Section, October to November 1916.

there were indeed baths at Meaulte.[149] Whether the men of the infantry divisions at the front had much time for baths is a moot question; they had so much to do.

Camp Life

When the troops were not working or re-building their camps the army would not let them sit still for long, not normally that is. Training and physical fitness was of paramount importance. Major-General Robertson was not going to allow his division to become slack and on 4 October, after a conference with all brigade and battalion commanders, while the division was up at Gommecourt, he had a number of orders issued throughout the division. The soldier's best friend was (and is) the rifle and practicing the art of shooting, or musketry as the British Army liked to call it, had to carry on regardless. The order about musketry read,

> *Musketry training must be continued vigorously. Men who are backward must be put through again. A good supply of dummy cartridges (2000 per Bn.) is essential. Teaching by demonstration and not merely by the book is most necessary.[150]*

Therefore musketry was practiced at the camps regardless of the weather as the formations adhered to their orders.[151] Physical training carried on in the mud,[152] and inspections were regular features of camp life.[153] Parades were commonplace although as

---

149 C. P. Blacker & J. Blacker (Ed), *Have You Forgotten Yet? The First World War Memoirs of C. P. Blacker, MC, GM,* (First published, Leo Cooper, 2000. Re-published, Pen & Sword, 2015), p. 140

150 TNA: PRO. WO 95/1981. War Diary, 17th Division, Appendices, October 1916.

151 TNA: PRO. WO 95/2002. War Diary, 7th East Yorks, October 1916. & TNA: PRO. WO 95/2004. War Diary, 50th Brigade Machine Gun Company, October 1916.

152 TNA: PRO. WO 95/2014. War Diary, 52nd Brigade Machine Gun Company, October 1916.

153 TNA: PRO. WO 95/2007. War Diary, 8th South Staffords, October 1916.

Captain Mozley wrote, "Company parades were frequently interrupted by rain."[154] Up at Divisional H.Q. close order drill was considered important and, among orders for tactical training, leap frog attacks and the need to train for co-operation with creeping barrages, the order about close order drill read,

Close order drill must not degenerate into a task to fill up time. Briskness and quick changes are the essence of good drill and the men must smarten up to it. Officers must continuously and vigorously correct every mistake. The quick gymnastic step is to be used. The drill must be constantly varied and made as interesting as possible.[155]

Although none of the units of the 17th Division recorded carrying out any close order drill while they were in these camps. Sensibly they waited until they were out of the line and away from the atrocious conditions, the heavy work load and tours in the front line.[156] On occasion the weather was so bad that the troops just remained under cover. On 30 October Lieutenant-Colonel Fife wrote a typical weather report, "Dull and windy, increasing to a gale with floods of rain in the afternoon. Did nothing."[157]

The conditions were ideal for causing all manner of sickness, disease and skin problems. Trench Foot was the one most dreaded by the battalions. Used as a marker of a battalion's efficiency the disease was, let alone the pain and discomfort it caused the sufferers, unwelcome because it attracted staff attention. If a battalion had a high number of cases then the staff believed that the men had given up caring about their own hygiene and ergo would give up caring for their kit and for offensive operations. It could also have serious consequences

---

[154] I IWM: Mozley, 01/48/1.
[155] TNA: PRO. WO 95/1981. War Diary, 17th Division, Appendices, October 1916.
[156] TNA: PRO. WO 95/2004. War Diary, 50th Brigade Machine Gun Company, November 1916.
[157] Personal diary of Lieutenant-Colonel Fife.

for the battalion commanders' careers as the 10[158] West Yorks were to discover.[158]

Here in the ocean of mud, lashed by freezing rain and sleet, it was very difficult to avoid Trench Foot let alone keep up the offensive spirit. R.A.M.C doctors from the Field Ambulances toured the camps lecturing the men on the Trench Foot condition,[159] however, better boots might have served to improve matters far more than words. Whale oil was sent up to the front in waterproof bags, the men rubbed this oil into their feet whenever they had the chance or were ordered to and they were advised to change into dry socks whenever possible.[160] However, the soldiers of the division had been on the march from camp to camp in dreadful weather and it was taking its toll on them, their boots, their socks, their feet and their kit. Captain Mozley, recalled,

As a result of all this marching, the men's boots were in a very bad state, and it was a difficult job getting new pairs for everyone … Kit inspections were held … anti-frostbite grease was issued and foot rubbing parades were started. [161]

Trench Foot was troubling the 6th Dorsets greatly and the fact that they were trying to combat the disease was recorded in their war diary, "It was practically impossible to get dry or clean, or to arrange any proper medical aid post [in the camps] to attend to the men's feet, which were naturally in a very bad condition."[162] The 6th Dorsets' Trench Foot statistics were not improved by

158 On 1 July this battalion suffered so many casualties, including the C.O and 2 i/c, that it very nearly ceased to exist as a unit. Major Gilbert Horsman Soames of the 1st West Yorks, who had served as a boy in the Lancashire Fusiliers in the Boer War, arrived to take over on 26 July and was promoted to Lieutenant-Colonel. To all intents and purposes he had managed to bring the battalion back up to strength but it would seem that the battalion had not recovered its morale.

159 TNA: PRO. WO 95/1996. War Diary, 51st Field Ambulance, R.E, October to November 1916.

160 Miles, *Official History, 1916*, Vol II, p. 537

161 IWM: Mozley, 01/48/1.

162 TNA: PRO WO 95/2000. War Diary, 6th Dorsets, October to November 1916.

the arrival at their camp of a new draft from Britain. "The incidence of trench feet was increased by the arrival of eighty-two reinforcements that had been trained to bicycles in Ireland and were altogether unfit for the rigours of the Somme."[163] The new boys were not used to marching everywhere and the Somme battlefield in October/November 1916 was no place by bicycles.

The 10th West Yorks' war diary tells posterity that all was well with the battalion in late October and the men were marching and training as well as could be expected. However, a large number of these men were new to the Western Front. [164] They were toughening up though because few, if any, fell out of route marches. On 23 October the whole battalion was lectured on the subject of Trench Foot and its prevention.[165] Yet in early November Trench Foot was rife throughout the battalion.

Everyone knew that the key to beating Trench Foot was to keep feet warm, clean and dry but, "A few braziers of coke [in the camps] were the only means of getting dry and clean. Cases of trench feet were frequent."[166] No one could keep their feet dry, clean or warm, not in mud that could come up to one's waist or be bottomless, or in water that came up to one's knees.[167] No matter how well dubbed the leather boots were they and the

---

[163] O' Hanlon, *A Plain History of the Sixth (Service) Battalion*, p. 125

[164] The battalions of the 17th Division, like most battalions which served in the opening phase of the Somme Campaign had lost large numbers of their original Kitchener Volunteers, either wounded or killed. During an attack upon Fricourt, on 1 July 1916, the 10th West Yorks had suffered extremely heavy casualties (including the C.O and the 2 i/c) and by October 1916 had been re-constituted with new drafts. A quick glance at the casualties for the battalion's first stint in the line at the end of October suggests that over half of the men which went into the front line on the night of 29 October had never been in combat before. They were stiffened by only a few survivors from July 1916 and veterans, like Privates William Ashton and Andrew Warringham, who had served in Gallipoli. Other newcomers to the battalion had been soldiers for some time but they had been in Britain it seems and had not seen active service. Only four of the casualties in this first stint in the line had been original Kitchener Volunteers. For further information see later on in this chapter and Appendix 02 Casualties.

[165] TNA: PRO. WO 95/2004. War Diary, 10th West Yorks, October 1916.

[166] O' Hanlon, *A Plain History of the Sixth (Service) Battalion*, p. 125

[167] TNA: PRO. WO 95/2000. War Diary, 6th Dorsets, October to November 1916.

woollen puttees tightly wrapped around the men's lower legs could not keep out the water, the cold or the dirt. In fact the puttees restricted circulation and the troops soon learned to wrap sandbags around their lower legs instead;[168] these were warmer and less restricting but they still did not keep out the water. Spare and dry socks were at a premium and sometimes soldiers were not averse to rifling through the contents of a dead comrade's pack to try and find socks. The Engineers had orders to build drying sheds for clothing at the camps but as has been seen they had plenty of other construction work on before the sheds could be built.[169]

The everyday the running of the division, brigades, battalions, companies, platoons and sections also occupied time; new drafts arrived and had to be assigned to companies, and personnel matters had to be attended to. Personnel changes, promotions and postings were going on all of the time in the division. At the beginning of November, Colonel O. R. A. Julian, R.A.M.C., was promoted to D.D.M.S. in the Cavalry Corps and Colonel H. P. W. Barrow, R.A.M.C.,[170] was promoted to Julian's former role as A.D.M.S in the 17th Division.[171] Not all postings were welcomed however, Lieutenant-Colonel Edward Lake Gowlland, R.A.M.C.,[172] the C.O., of the 51st Field Ambulance grumbled that,

---

[168] Miles, *Official History, 1916*, Vol II, p. 537

[169] TNA: PRO. WO 95/1993. War Diary, 78th Field Company, R.E., October to November 1916.

[170] Barrow had come out to the Western Front on 2 November 1914 as a major. He was later promoted to Colonel. He was Mentioned in Despatches on 25 January 1917, 29 May 1917 and 24 December 1917. On 2 January 1918 he was ruled ineligible for the 1914 Star and in 1920 was only issued with the British War Medal and Victory Medal.

[171] TNA: PRO. WO 95/1989. War Diary, A.D.M.S., November 1916.

[172] Gowlland, a Territorial Force Medical Officer, came out to the Western Front with his unit in July 1915 as a major and was promoted to Lieutenant-Colonel. He was Mentioned in Despatches on 1 January 1916 and 29 May 1917. In 1920 Gowlland was working for the Ministry of Pensions in Room 66, Burton Court, Kings Road, London.

Captain M. E. Gorman, RAMC, removed from this unit and posted to 12th Labour Battalion, the Black Watch, we thus lose the services of one of the best bearer officers it is possible to have, who has been with the unit since its arrival in this country and who knows every man in the unit, and thus to go as MO in charge a Labour BN...[173]

It was pointless for Lieutenant-Colonel Gowlland to complain, Captain Gorman's orders had been issued by XIV Corps. Gorman was replaced by Captain McVickers.[174]

At the end of October the 17th Division's senior Veterinarian, Major W. W. R. Neale A.D.V.S.,[175] had to deal with a couple of personnel issues. Before the 17th Division transferred to the Fourth Army, Captain F. K. Henton, A.V.C.,[176] was reported by the O.C. of No. 4 Company, 17th Divisional Train for his poor behaviour and the incident attracted the attention of the D.D.V.S of Third Army. Major Neale visited Third Army H.Q. to discuss the matter and on the following day the D.D.V.S., Colonel Hunt, arrived at Neale's unit to interview Henton himself. Following the interview Colonel Hunt and Major Neale visited the 17th Divisional Train and carried out an inspection of their own. It appears that no punishment was metered out to Henton.[177] It is easy to imagine that the veterinarian Henton had a disagreement with the O.C., 4th Company, 17th Divisional Train about the health of the unit's horses. The D.D.V.S., and Neale probably upheld their colleague's point of view. While Colonel

---

[173] TNA: PRO. WO 95/1996. War Diary, 51st Field Ambulance, October – November 1916.

[174] TNA: PRO. WO 95/1989. War Diary, A.D.M.S., November 1916.

[175] Major Neale, a regular army veterinarian, had come out with the B.E.F., as a captain, A.V.S., on 16 August 1914. He was soon promoted to major and was Mentioned in Despatches on 22 June 1916, 15 May 1917 and 20 December 1918. After the war he served in India and rose to the rank of Lieutenant-Colonel.

[176] A regular army veterinarian who arrived on the Western Front on 23 September 1914 as a lieutenant.

[177] TNA: PRO. WO 95/1990. War Diary, A.D.V.S., October 1916.

Hunt was in the divisional area he also inspected the 29th Mobile Veterinary Section and was pleased with what he saw.[178]

After the 17th Division had transferred to Fourth Army, Major Neale had been forced to report Acting Sergeant 5379 Isaac Batt as inefficient and negligent in his duties. The D.D.V.S. of Fourth Army visited Neale in person to discuss the sergeant's behaviour and possible punishment. It was decided to demote the man and get rid of him by sending him to work at a Veterinary Hospital. By the time the officers had decided Batt's fate he had been wounded,[179] admitted to hospital and could not be demoted. They managed to get rid of him though, because he was transferred to the Royal Field Artillery. [180]

On 29 October, as the 7th Yorks sat in their soggy camp, an irritated Lieutenant-Colonel Fife also had personnel problems. He wrote, reminding us at first of the weather,

A wild and very wet morning. Dickson (Qr. Mr.)[181] sent to Field Ambulance with bad cold. As he is always going sick with something or other I have recommended his transfer to Home Service.[182]

He had done this before, to another officer, recorded simply as 'Young', earlier in the war. The officer had taken to his bed through illness and Lieutenant-Colonel Fife sent him packing.

---

178 TNA: PRO. WO 95/1997. War Diary, 29th Mobile Veterinary Section, October 1916.

179 He was later awarded the Silver War Badge.

180 TNA: PRO. WO 95/1990. War Diary, A.D.V.S., 17th Division, October 1916 & Medal Index Card. Interestingly, after the war, Batt's name appears on his Medal Index Card on a list of prisoners names forwarded for war medals by the Military Police.

181 Lieutenant Thomas Johnstone Dickson, Yorkshire Regiment, the Green Howards, arrived in France as a second lieutenant in 1916. His arrival at the battalion is not recorded in the war diary but he may have been one of 8 un-named second lieutenants who joined on 21 June 1916. His promotion to lieutenant and elevation to the post of Quartermaster are not mentioned in the war diary either. Of his evacuation there is no mention in the war diary, or in Fife's diary. Only the divisional Quartermaster General noted his evacuation. Lieutenant Dickson survived the war. Medal Index Card and TNA: PRO. WO 95/2004. War Diary, 7th Yorks, June 1916.

182 Personal diary of Lieutenant-Colonel Fife.

It would appear that Lieutenant-Colonel Fife did not have an issue with men or officers being sick or ill, what he took exception to was officers *going sick* or to put it another way, doing no work and taking to their beds or, even worse, being admitted to the hospital sick. It was not something he did himself; even when ill he tried to keep working and thereby remained at his post. It was his standard for his battalion. Hence Dickson, like Young before him, was sent home. Fife's main symptoms were always the same and he was ill quite often; a chill, headaches, shivers and feeling 'seedy' or weak. He also recorded neuralgic and rheumatic pain and at one point lost his voice. The periods of illness lasted about a week and he decided each time that he had Influenza or a cold and left it at that.[183]

Lieutenant T. J. Dickson was actually considered ill enough to be evacuated to Britain on 1 November 1916.[184] Perhaps Fife was being too harsh because men were regularly going sick, draining the units of manpower as surely as an offensive did. Considering the workload and conditions it was hardly surprising. The chief causes for admission to hospital for soldiers, other than wounds, at this time in 1916, were Trench Foot, Frostbite, Nephritis, Dysentery, Rubella and Venereal Disease.[185]

Nephritis is an inflammation of the kidneys and the upper urinary tract. The symptoms are swelling around the face, ankles, feet and hands, high blood pressure, fatigue and aching pain on one or both sides of the lower back and in the stomach. Given the latter symptoms the army of 1916 can be forgiven for thinking that this illness was caused by "cold and humidity, hard work and overloading the soldier with heavy equipment."[186] The actual cause is a bacterial infection from a backward flow of

183 Lieutenant-Colonel Fife's personal diary.
184 TNA: PRO. WO 95/1986. War Diary, Adjutant & Quartermaster General, 17th Division, November 1916.
185 Miles, *Official History, 1916, Vol II*, p 537
186 Miles, *Official History, 1916, Vol II*, p 537

urine from the bladder into the upper urinary tract. The best way to avoid Nephritis is to drink often, to urinate often and practice good hygiene., none of which activities were easy for soldiers to do in the line or in the camps. Fresh drinking water was an issue, hence the orders for the Engineers to lay pipelines to the camps and often tea was made with water from shell holes, not the cleanest of sources of water. In the rear areas water could be got from standpipes if they had been installed or from wells in the ruined villages, if they had not been destroyed in the fighting or contaminated by chemicals or dead bodies. Otherwise water was carried to where it was needed in used two gallon petrol cans.[187] They were not hygienic containers by any stretch of the imagination but the Medical Services did their best to ensure that safe water was provided. Lieutenant-Colonel Barrow the A.D.M.S., wrote,

Owing to the fact that cases of Dysentery have occurred in the Division, it is of paramount importance that all water used by the troops should be chlorinated or boiled before use.

Medical Officers in charge of units will, from time to time, test samples of water used for drinking and cooking purposes, by the troops under their medical charge, and will issue instructions as to the degree of chlorination required before use.[188]

Some soldiers were fussy about going to the toilet in the line, no one wanted to get hit while going to the toilet so there was a tendency for some soldiers to 'hold it' until they got to a latrine.[189] Hygiene was practically impossible until one found a proper washroom and in October – November 1916 they were in the process of being constructed in the camps and, once again, water was an issue. None of the trenches or dugouts were equipped with wash basins and there was no running water in

---

[187] Miles, *Official History, 1916, Vol II*, p 540

[188] TNA: PRO. WO 95/1989. War Diary, A.D.M.S., November 1916.

[189] Imperial War Museum (IWM): Unpublished papers Sapper and later Colonel F. Palmer Cook, O.B.E., T.D. 81/44/1.

the trenches either.[190] Trips to the baths at Meaulte would have been a rare treat in November 1916. The construction, function and cleanliness of urinals, latrines and bath houses were all in the remit of the Sanitary Section. Their works and work was supervised and inspected by medical staff from the A.D.M.S.' department and the Field Ambulances.

It was not just humans who suffered wounds and sickness from the conditions and poor hygiene. Once they were settled at Mansell Copse the Vets spent a good deal of time looking after and treating sick horses and mules. Those that they could not help at their base were evacuated by rail to the No. 7 Veterinary Hospital. This kind of work took the Veterinarians away from the area because someone had to be with the animals being transported; it also meant that they were not available to treat animals at the camp. Often the commander of the Section, South African Vet Captain J. J. G. Keppel, A.V.S.,[191] would be on one of these trips along with a number of attendants, both NCOs and other ranks.[192] As time went on the list of animal casualties rose; a typical war diary entry for a day in November read,

47 animals evacuated to No. 7 Veterinary Hospital, 3 animals (horses) destroyed in section from Debility. Animals being in a most

---

190 Water was supplied from boring plants at Amiens and wells in the villages. Pipelines did stretch forward and at the height of the campaign water was provided for 150,000 animals and 300,000 soldiers. Water was also carried forward by road. Water pipes, standpipes and wells were often hit by artillery rounds and the roads were always congested; the further forward one went it became harder to find or receive fresh water. Miles, *Official History, 1916, Vol II*, p. 540.

191 Keppel was a regular army veterinarian and had arrived on the Western Front on 28 August 1914. He was Mentioned in Despatches in 1917 and later awarded the O.B.E., for his work during the Great War. Keppel returned to his native Transvaal after the war.

192 TNA: PRO. WO 95/1997. War Diary, 29th Mobile Veterinary Section, October 1916.

emaciated condition and unable to rise off the ground where they lay. 9 animals admitted sick.[193]

Those numbers rose as hungry, mangy, lame and sick animals arrived at the camp, some were treated on site, others evacuated to the hospital, and occasionally some were shot.[194] In November, over a nineteen day period, the Veterinary Section admitted 230 sick horses and mules to the camp for treatment and assessment. Three hundred and fifteen animals were evacuated to hospital over the same period, some of these were sent on to hospital immediately without waiting for treatment at the camp which explains the unbalanced number. On one day alone the Vets evacuated 54 horses and mules to hospital.

Overseeing the welfare of the division's animals, Captain Keppel's commanding officer, Major Neale, remarked in the War Diary for November that,

During the month the hay ration was reduced to 8 lbs per animal per day. Number of cases of 'picked up nail'[195] in forward area very large. Number of cases of 'necrotic ulcer'[196] very much on the increase. Watering of animals in the forward area very difficult owing to the comparatively few water places and the journey through mud. Large number of shoes pulled by the mud. Owing to the large number of animals requiring evacuation in the forward area the personnel of the M.V.S.[197] was insufficient to deal with them and supply conducting parties by rail. A large proportion of the sick animals came from Corps

---

193 TNA: PRO. WO 95/1997. War Diary, 29th Mobile Veterinary Section, November 1916.

194 TNA: PRO. WO 95/1997. War Diary, 29th Mobile Veterinary Section, November 1916.

195 Horses' hooves are susceptible to being punctured by sharp objects and the battlefield, the roads and Horse Lines were littered with long, sharp objects. Sometimes the object remained in the wound, and sometimes the object remained where it was on the ground. Swift action was needed if infection, disease and unnecessary suffering was to be avoided. The wounds and abscesses had to be cleaned, drained and poultices applied and the animal had to be rested.

196 Abscesses.

197 Mobile Veterinary Service, in this instance the 29th Mobile Section.

Troops and these having no M.V.S. have to be cleared by divisional M.V.S. [198]

Sometimes there were not enough railway vehicles available to take all of the animals so they had to be taken back to the camp. As Major Neale had remarked sending animals to the hospital depleted the Mobile Section's personnel so it was usual for one attendant to care for three animals at the camp. Like their medical colleagues in the R.A.M.C., the Vets and their attendants did a remarkable job of work. Remember these figures are just for one division and there were many divisions on the Somme in October and November 1916 and all arms used horses and mules. The Vets and their attendants were always busy and it is testimony to the dedicated work of the 29th Mobile Section that over this same nineteen day period only seven animals had to be shot and only one died of illness in their care.[199]

It is small wonder that the Vets were so busy, the work that the horses and mules had to do was very heavy and strenuous. Guns had a voracious appetite for shells putting enormous strain on the men and animals that supplied them. By and large the men who worked with the animals grew deeply attached to their charges and the 81st (Howitzer) Brigade, R.F.A., C.O., Lieutenant-Colonel R. S. Hardman,[200] left a pen portrait of the 17th Division's artillery horses,

> *I must say a word of the merits of the North American horses we were fortunate to get … He was the best of all draught horses it has ever been my fortune to have had to deal with … small, few of them over 15.2, symmetrical, round, standing on short legs, with good feet, he had all the virtues of the equine race, with few of its faults. He seemed to*

---

[198] TNA: PRO. WO 95/1990. War Diary, A.D.V.S., 17th Division, November 1916.

[199] TNA: PRO. WO 95/1997. War Diary, 29th Mobile Veterinary Section, October – November, 1916.

[200] Lieutenant-Colonel Hardman had been a regular artillery major when he went out the Western Front on 9 September 1914 and was sent back to Britain in early 1915 to be promoted and to form the 81st (Howitzer) Brigade within the 17th Division. He was Mentioned in Despatches three times, 15 February 1915, 15 June 1916 and 4 January 1917. He survived the war.

revel in hardship. Mud, wet, neglect and short fare, a most honest worker. I seldom, if ever, saw a team gibbing. At the same time he was extraordinarily docile, tame and easy to handle.[201]

To save their animals the strain of hard work there were attempts to use methods of delivery other than horses and mules. The 17th Divisional Ammunition Column[202] C.O., Lieutenant-Colonel Robert William Layard Dunlop[203] wrote,

The difficulties of supplying ammunition to gun positions are very great owing to the absence of roads and the presence of deep mud. It has been found practically impossible to supply by limbers, even using teams of ten or twelve horses or mules has been such a strain on the animals that this practice has been discontinued. A tramline exists and passes close to certain battery positions and wherever possible this tramline has been used to supply these batteries. The distance others are from the nearest place on the tramline renders it a doubtful advantage to them. It has been found from experience that the tramline is only useable to a certain point and that some batteries are a very considerable distance from this point.[204]

If mechanical means failed then the animals had to be called upon again. Lieutenant-Colonel Dunlop continued,

Experiments have been tried in adapting the saddle into a sort of pack saddle for the carrying of ammunition to the gun positions and the most useful way has been to strap or tie two boxes to the saddle, one on each side, thus carrying eight rounds 18pdr per horse and four rounds 4.5" per horse direct to the guns from the dump. Thus the four horses

---

201 Atteridge, *The History of the 17th (Northern) Division*, p. 22

202 This ammunition column was serving other artillery brigades at the time but their experiences are worth noting.

203 Regular Artilleryman Lieutenant-Colonel Dunlop had gone out to the Western Front with the 17th Division on 15 July 1915 and during his service he was awarded the D.S.O and a Mention in Despatches on 18 May 1917. After the war he worked in the Legislative Department of the Government of India as the Solicitor to the Government of India. He was also the honorary Colonel of the Bombay Volunteer Rifles.

204 TNA: PRO. WO 95/1992. War Diary, 17th Divisional Ammunition Column, October - November 1916.

formerly put in a wagon limber, which holds 38 rounds 18 pdr or 16 rounds 4.5" have been made to take 80 rounds – 18pdr or 40 rounds 4.5".[205]

With animals being used for all manner of transport work in heavy and deep mud, let alone travelling slowly through shellfire there were bound to be mounting casualties.

Of course the artillery was always close at hand, in fact there were guns everywhere and they added to the discomfort of the camp dwellers. Lieutenant-Colonel Fife wrote, "A 15-inch howitzer is in action close to this camp and makes a hideous noise."[206] Captain O'Hanlon recalled that "a worn out 15-inch gun firing rapid four rounds per hour towards Bapaume (the rocking shell could be followed by eye) shook the mud from the sides of the holes the men lived in."[207] Not only did they attract the lethal attention of their counterparts from the German side of the line, their noise and vibration had an impact on all aspects daily and nightly life.

Everyday domestic arrangements and transport issues along with the awful weather and ground conditions worried Lieutenant-Colonel Nicholson who was based with his Advanced Echelon at Bernafay Wood.[208] "Almost all supplies of food, water, ammunition and material had to be taken to forward dump by pack animal." However, the division did not have enough animals and had to borrow a 100 mules from Corps in order to maintain the levels of supply. Laundry was a concern, particularly from a health point of view. No provision had been made by either Army or Corps for laundry; a division arriving in the sector was expected to make its own arrangements and improvise. Consequently, the division set up a small laundry at

---

[205] TNA: PRO. WO 95/1992. War Diary, 17th Divisional Ammunition Column, October - November 1916.

[206] Personal diary of Lieutenant-Colonel Fife.

[207] O' Hanlon, *A Plain History of the Sixth (Service) Battalion*, p. 125

[208] The Rear Echelon of the divisional Quartermaster branch with further stores was based at Minden Post alongside the 17th Division H.Q.

Ville but it was woefully inadequate to fulfil the needs of an infantry division. Nicholson and his staff solved the problem by simply issuing new clothing to the troops as they needed it and storing the dirty clothing as salvage for washing and renovation at a later date. Warm food and drink was vital to the troops so Nicholson's staff established Soup Kitchens at the camps to provide a ready source of sustenance whenever it was needed.[209] Hot cocoa was also provided by the divisional canteen for those who were lucky enough to be in the vicinity and the battalion kitchens served up hot Bovril at all times of day and night.[210]

Food was something that was never far from the soldiers' minds. After being collected from the dump Rations were carried forward in sand bags and generally consisted of bully beef, biscuits or Maconochies.[211] Sometimes there was hard, mouldy bread and cheese, other times bacon and it was more often than not carried in the same bags. By the time that the food was doled out everything had become mixed and mashed up in the sand bags. Rum was kept in stone jars marked S.R.D,[212] which the Tommies translated as "Seldom Reaches Destination", and was entrusted to an N.C.O.[213] Sapper F. Palmer Cook of the 78th Field Company, R.E, remembered that when the troops had to cook for themselves, a good meal could be had by cooking up bully beef, crushed biscuits and a dash of precious H.P. Sauce in a mess tin. Mess tins were scrubbed clean with gritty turf pulled from the ground. He recalled that the strong Army tea was brewed in dixies with tins of sweetened condensed milk added and handfuls of sugar thrown in. It was a welcome brew at any

---

209 TNA: PRO. WO 95/1986. War Diary, Assistant Adjutant and Quarter Master General, 17th Division, October - November 1916.

210 TNA: PRO. WO 95/2000. War Diary, 6th Dorsets, October to December 1916.

211 This was a tinned stew of potatoes, turnips and carrots in a thin soup and so named after the Scottish company that produced it. To say it was unpopular with the troops is an understatement.

212 Service Ration Department.

213 IWM: Mozley, 01/48/1.

time of day or night,[214] when rum was added it was called 'gunfire'.

Even at the front pay was important. On the afternoon of 28 October Captain Mozley decided to pay the men of A Company. He knew that the battalion was due to go forward soon and he had no desire to go into the line with a large amount of money in his possession; nor did he want the company books to show a large balance at the start of the month. His colleague Captain Charles Hamilton Leigh Kindersley,[215] the CO of D Company opted to pay his men on the following morning.[216]

Later that evening there was a concert at the camp held in the Church Army hut.[217] It was warm, dry, no doubt diverting and A Company went along with money in their pockets. D Company went along with none and to add insult to injury on the following morning they were ordered forward to the front line; there was no time to pay D Company. Captain Kindersley "had to take hundreds of francs with him into the trenches,"[218] along with his (possibly) disgruntled company.

The Road To The Line

Battalions from the 17th Division began to go into the line on the night of 29/30 October as the formation began the relief of the 8th Division. On the right the 50th Brigade had two battalions in the line and two in support. In the centre the 51st Brigade had one battalion in the line and one in support. On the left the 52nd Brigade had two battalions in the line and two in support. With

---

[214] IWM: Cook, 81/44/1.

[215] Charles Hamilton Leigh Kindersley later served in Iraq, promoted to major and was awarded the G.S.M.

[216] IWM: Mozley, 01/48/1. Mozely recorded that this happened on 27 October but the battalion war diary states that it was 28 October.

[217] TNA: PRO. WO 95/2000. War Diary, 6th Dorsets, October to November 1916.

[218] IWM: Mozley, 01/48/1.

the 17th Division's artillery operating in another part of the Somme line they were covered by the divisional artillery from the Guards, the 4th and 20th Divisions.[219] The 17th Division H.Q. was set up at the hut camp at Bernafay Wood on 31 October.[220]

The trek to the front line and the ground conditions that the troops encountered were truly worse than anything that the veterans had so far experienced in the war. It made a deep impression on the men and many tried to record their experience to preserve it for posterity. The Staff Officers at Brigade, Divisional and Corps H.Qs were well aware of the conditions faced by the troops. One of the three Brigade commanders, Glasgow, Trotter, or Clarke, wrote about the troops' approach to the front line for the divisional history; bafflingly A. Hilliard Atteridge, the author of that tome, failed to identify which brigadier-general it was. The general wrote,

It was impossible to transport blankets for them, so the troops had only greatcoats and groundsheets wherewith to withstand the wintry conditions that had already set in … Longueval had been flattened into heaps of bricks and rubble but what a different scene [was Delville Wood] to my last acquaintance with that accursed spot! Now there was scarcely a vestige of wood left – a few trunks of not more than four or five feet high, the rest tree stumps and shell holes jostling one another, with a duckboard walk zig-zagging its way to the northern edge, when it traversed a downward sloping crater field until a hollow valley was reached, into the opposite slope of which dugouts had been tunnelled; away from the duckboards nothing but mud, shell holes and debris. It was a scene of abomination and desolation indeed, with barely a vestige of life or movement visible to the eye on the surface, though not so in the air where the bursts of shrapnel and 'archies'[221] were continually in

---

219 Atteridge, *History of the 17th (Northern) Division*, p. 168 - 169

220 Atteridge, *History of the 17th (Northern) Division*, p. 168

221 Air burst anti-aircraft shells.

evidence, with occasionally the dull thud of an H.E. shell, throwing up its geyser of mud, stones and debris.[222]

Lieutenant Hoyte also recorded his experience of approaching the front line,

The main road through Mametz and Montauban, up which all the supplies of a large part of the front had to travel, was in an appalling state; it never appeared to have been properly mended since its capture in July and now the whole of the metalled surface was a mass of pasty gravel, churned up into ruts sometimes a couple of feet deep, while the wheels of the transport rested in the slimy chalk underneath. Farther forward there were merely trackless deserts of the altogether indescribable Somme mud. A straggling line of duckboards went forward from Waterlot Farm, near Guillemont; some of these were floating, some tipped on one side, some just upset the unwary walker for no apparent reason. After a mile of these boards on which one performed feats worthy of Blondin,[223] they ceased, and one pushed out into the void…[224]

Such were the appalling ground conditions and horrendous weather that platoons straggled into the line along the torturous route. When the 6th Dorsets went into the line Captain Mozley was forced to go back from the front line to find his lost platoons and guide them in personally. It was not their fault, they were heavily laden with equipment and the mud and rain, sleet and hail, darkness and exhausted guides,[225] who did not

---

[222] Reconstruction of a narrative written by an un-named 17th Division Brigadier-General in Atteridge, *History of the 17th (Northern) Division,* p. 169 – 70. It is possible that the words were written by Brigadier-General Glasgow of 50th Brigade because he mentions Delville Wood and the 50th Brigade had its H.Q. there at this time.

[223] The Great Charles Blondin (real name Jean-Francois Gravelet) was a famous French acrobat and tightrope walker who performed death defying feats to admiring audiences in North America and in the United Kingdom. He popularised tightrope walking and acrobatics and a number of other acrobats performed under the name Blondin. Gravelet died in Ealing in 1897, aged 72. It is a mark of Blondin's popularity and fame that Hoyte still referred to him when writing about the 10th Notts & Derbys just after the war's end.

[224] Hoyte, *10th (S) Battalion,* p. 21 - 22

[225] Much has been said about poor guides, they are often grumbled about in memoirs, diaries and the unit war diaries and they are often blamed by incoming battalions

know the way to the line, all conspired to slow the men down. Of course, there was always the artillery, the German gunners had their way of slowing things down as well. Lieutenant Hoyte wrote, "The enemy artillery added to the general hellishness of the situation."[226] Trench reliefs were an agony and Captain Mozley remembered the route to the line and his battalion's first relief of an 8th Division battalion. He wrote that it,

> ...almost beggars description. The route to the trenches lay through Guillemont and Ginchy, and after passing through the ruins of the latter place we found ourselves on an open waste, unsurpassed for desolation. As far as the eye could reach, a brown shell-pocked plain spread before us, devoid of landmarks. Villages had been reduced to heaps of rubble, and woods to jagged blackened stumps. Our course, according to the map, was a North Easterly one, through T8 Central, which later on was the map reference for a big dump of supplies and ammunition. Away to our right, the ruins of Morval could be seen, surmounting a hill which rose more abruptly than usual from the general level of the ground. Les Boeufs [sic] itself will be chiefly remembered by its sunken roads, which were full of mud which surpassed anything previously encountered.[227]

In the Line

For some of the troops there was little gap in between arrival on the Somme and going into the front line. The 10th West Yorks were one such battalion and their early four day tour in the line was a horror. On 29 October, two days after arriving on the

---

for delayed reliefs. Guides were provided by the outgoing battalion and the truth was that these men had often had an intense tour of duty in the line and were sometimes hungry, wet, exhausted and dispirited. Also, this part of the line was difficult to navigate to, from and around. Land marks were few in the sea of mud, trenches were not always visible and it was easy to lose one's direction or take a wrong turn. Doing this in the dark made things even more difficult. This is why Captain Mozley navigated by the stars when he could.

226 Hoyte, *10th (S) Battalion*, p. 22

227 IWM: Mozley, 01/48/1.

Somme, they had gone into the front line, to be specific the portion of Zenith Trench held by the British, and the support and reserve trenches. Zenith Trench was an important position because, until its complete capture by the British, this trench was actually held by both sides as part of their respective front lines.

Two men, Fred Gott and Robert Hanley were killed by shelling as the battalion began the relief of the 2nd West Yorks, 8th Division, on the night of 29 October. On arrival in the front line trenches Sergeant Dickson did manage to take a wounded German solider of the 28th Reserve Infantry Reserve Regiment prisoner.

The ground conditions were shocking. Rain and shelling were incessant for four days and after the peaceful, late summer days at Gommecourt it was a harsh return to the war. The 10th West Yorks' duty was to hold the line and the impossible tasks, in view of the shelling, rain and the bottomless mud, of consolidating the trenches and connecting Zenith to the British trenches.

The war diary recorded,

> *Weather conditions were deplorable, men in the front trenches having to stand at least two feet in mud water. Several men became stuck in the mud – were unable to move until they were dug out. Shelling was continuous and caused considerable casualties.*[228]

The battalion did not patrol or raid or go onto the offensive and in the main the casualties were caused by shellfire. The ration parties were sniped and shelled therefore food and water were scarce. Orderly, Private H. Neale captured the German soldier Ludwig Huber on 2 November confirming the presence of the 28th Reserve Infantry Regiment. [229] Apart from Dickenson and Neale's small successes, the battalion simply 'took it' for no reply. It was a severe shock to the unit which had not had a

---

[228] TNA: PRO. WO 95/2004. War Diary, 10th West Yorks, October 1916.
[229] TNA: PRO. WO 95/2004. War Diary, 10th West Yorks, October & November 1916.

combat casualty since August and which had been in a quiet sector for weeks. They were sitting targets for the German artillery and could do nothing in return.

On 3 November the keeper of the 10th West Yorks war diary wrote, "The Battalion marched to 'C' Camp, Mansel Camp. The men arrived in an exhausted state after the severe experiences in the trenches. Many were suffering from Trench Feet." [230] Considering the High Command's view of Trench Foot as a marker of morale, the large numbers of Trench Foot cases would have indicated to Brigade and Division that the 10th West Yorks' morale was falling. It was a state that they were not going to recover from during the month. According to the war diary the battalion suffered 85 casualties in this one tour; fourteen killed, two died of wounds, one officer gone sick[231] and 68 wounded.[232] However, the record keeping was incomplete and records show that 29 men were killed by shelling.[233] Given the experiences of the 10th West Yorks between 29 October and 3 November it was small wonder that their morale and physical health began to ebb right from the start of the 17th Division's tour.

As the situation in Zenith Trench demonstrated the trench line was chaotic and not easily defined. It was worrying for soldiers, used to secure trenches and who understood lines of support and reserve, to be faced with such uncertainty. Lieutenant-Colonel Fife noted at the time that, "The line seems to be very confused between here & Le Transloy. There is no wire in front of either our trenches or the Boches."[234] The battlefield was a sea of mud, and the trenches were not the deep, well-constructed German types of the early days of the campaign, they were not

---

230 TNA: PRO. WO 95/2004. War Diary, 10th West Yorks, November 1916.
231 This was Second Lieutenant J. H. Cloughly who was later on promoted to lieutenant and survived the war.
232 TNA: PRO. WO 95/2004. War Diary, 10th West Yorks, October & November 1916.
233 *Soldiers Died in the Great War* database.
234 Personal diary of Lieutenant-Colonel Fife.

even the rougher, less permanent British ones. Lines were made up of shell holes and slit trenches and isolated posts connected to a few deeper, narrow trenches. While there were some deeper dugouts in the support positions, usually in the sunken roads, dugouts in the line were small and few in number. Navigation was difficult; features were scarce in the wastes of no-man's-land and it was easy to become lost or fall into a mud filled hole. It was a disconnected front line and the chances of missing one's own positions and wandering into German held territory were high. Boundaries between units were porous and "It was no unusual experience for men of different divisions to get mixed up, and for parties of men to be adopted for some hours…"[235] If the British front line was a confused picture the Tommies knew that "the enemy front trench (Zenith Trench) overlooked a considerable part of our line, [51st Brigade] (Misty and Gusty Trenches)."[236] Although, as it turned out, when they went into the line no one in the 51st Brigade actually knew exactly where Zenith Trench was or how far it stretched. They just had a rough idea.

The mud in the trenches was deep; Lieutenant Hoyte wrote that it was, "Up to your middle and deeper, with no bottom to the stuff if anyone optimistically began to shovel it away."[237] Captain Mozley remembered A Company's first hours in the front line in this sector. As they had done in the camps, the soldiers tried to improve their positions by making them habitable. He also recalled trying to do his 'rounds',

We had very few tools, with which to improve our habitations but the next morning we made a start, to do the best we could. Rain fell heavily, however, and put the whole place in an awful state. The sides of the trench started to fall in, and the mud got deeper and deeper. There were no shelters of any sort, so that sleep was practically out of the question. We were not holding a very wide front, but the quality of the mud may

235 IWM: Mozley, 01/48/1.
236 Hoyte, *10th (S) Battalion*, p. 22
237 Hoyte, *10th (S) Battalion*, p. 22

be gauged by the fact that it took me the whole night to visit once every section in the company, and I was absolutely exhausted at the end of the round. I travelled over the top as much as possible, and with the minimum of equipment, but of course I had to traverse some portions of waterlogged trench. I sometimes thought, when I was pulling my legs one after the other out of the mud, that I should pull them out of joint.[238]

Mozley had been lucky not to be hit as he went out into the open but he seemed to lead a charmed life. Lieutenant-Colonel Fife noted the 50th Brigade's battalion commanders' trials as they attempted to tour the front line. Such was the shortage of dugouts that for a time during a relief four battalion commanders[239] shared one, tiny 5 feet by 9 feet H.Q. hole. Fife wrote,

I have never seen anything like the mud. Outside the hd. Qrs. dug-out it is more than knee deep and the C. O.s of E & W. York [s] both told me that they had tried in vain to go around the trenches. Soames, the W. York C.O.,[240] stuck fast and had to be pulled out … At about 6.am. Clive [the C.O., of the 7th East Yorks][241] started out to look at his trenches and being compelled by the mud to go along the top of the ground was shot in the arm and groin. He sent back word that the wound was slight and refused to be carried down until after dark. I assumed temporary command of his Battn.[242]

Lieutenant-Colonel Percy Archer Clive, M.P., was wise to remain where he was, to move him in daylight, labouring slow

---

238 IWM: Mozley, 01/48/1.

239 The COs of the 6th Dorsets, 10th West Yorks, 7th East Yorks and 7th Yorks.

240 Gilbert Horsman Soames had been a captain with the 1st West Yorks and went out to the Western Front on 28 June 1915. He was soon promoted to major and on 26 July 1916 he was promoted to Lieutenant-Colonel and took over what remained of the 10th West Yorks.

241 Percy Archer Clive had been the M.P. for Herefordshire since 1908 and was a captain in the 1st Grenadier Guards. He went out to the Western Front on 23 November 1914 but soon went back to Britain to take command, as a Lieutenant-Colonel, of the newly formed 7th East Yorks. Once his wounds had healed he went back out to France again, this time as the C.O. of the 1/5th Lancashire Fusiliers and was killed in action on 4 or 5 April 1918.

242 Personal diary of Lieutenant-Colonel Fife.

through the mud, would have invited serious injury or death for the stretcher-bearers and himself. Getting wounded men out of the line was difficult and dangerous and the journey from the aid posts was just as arduous. The Official History noted,

> *Stretcher-bearers, with never less than four men to a stretcher, made the journey down from the regimental aid posts through mud which no wheeled carrier could negotiate: but all that man could do was done to get the sick and wounded away with the minimum of exposure and suffering. The bearers of the field ambulances were often reinforced by pioneers, men from the divisional trains and others who could be spared. Prisoners on their way down from the front also assisted. The "carry" from Gueudecourt to Longueval, where the wounded were transferred to a tramway, was about 3,500 yards, divided into three stages.*[243]

Lieutenant-Colonel Clive's wounds were serious and word was sent back to the Transport Lines for the 7th East Yorks' 2 i/c to come forward and take command at 2.30 pm. Major G. East King[244] duly arrived at 7.30 pm and took over. At 33 years of age Lieutenant-Colonel Clive was a young and vigorous man and as such was a great loss to his battalion and the 50th Brigade.

Chances to be offensive and go onto the offensive did occasionally arise. Mozley recalled that on one of his nightly trips around his platoons,

> *One night I had just reached a Lewis Gun post, when we observed the dim shapes of a party of Germans in the darkness in front of us. The gun was not long in coming into action, but it jammed after one round, and the ghostly shapes had disappeared before it was in action again.*[245]

By and large being in the front line was all about holding the line and the main problem, apart from the conditions, was the

---

[243] Miles, *Official History, 1916, Vol II*, p. 537

[244] G. E. King had been a temporary captain when he joined the 7th East Yorks and he went out to the Western Front with them on 14 July 1915. He was Mentioned in Despatches on 4 January 1917, 22 May 1917 and 11 December 1917. He survived the war.

[245] IWM: Mozley, 01/48/1.

artillery. Shelling was not as heavy or intense as it had been in the earlier days of the campaign but it still took a toll of the men in the trenches. While in the line Captain Mozley and his officers had a close shave,

> *Not much shelling came our way, but one high velocity shell, perhaps a 4.2, was nearly the end of all the officers in "A" Coy. I was sitting, talking to the Platoon commanders, who all happened to be at one spot in the trench (which never should have occurred of course), when one of them bumped into me, and I realised that I was deaf. My ears were singing. The shell had exploded just behind the trench, and had deafened me before I could hear it explode. This must surely be very unusual. One man a few yards away received severe shell shock.*[246]

Mozley remained in the line with his company and within twenty-four hours his hearing had returned to normal. Mozley and 'A' Company had been lucky and he was lucky again when,

> *I was forced to prostrate myself hurriedly, a 5.9 bursting with a roar about 15 yards from me. No further shells came over, and, as it had been perfectly quiet all the time that I had been at H.Q., it looked exactly as if I had been spotted, and had been favoured with a shell for my especial benefit.*[247]

But, of course, shells could and did kill. Lieutenant August Agelasto, M.C., an officer of Greek descent, a veteran of the Balkan Wars and on secondment from the 1st Dorsets, was standing outside of the 6th Dorsets Battalion H.Q when a shell detonated nearby. It blew off both of his legs and killed him.[248]

Mozley wrote vividly about the sound of French 75 mm artillery bombardment fired from the right of the line while he and his men were in the front line,

> *An intense strafe was started by our guns away on the right. A very heavy shrapnel barrage was laid down, which seemed to indicate an*

---

[246] IWM: Mozley, 01/48/1.

[247] IWM: Mozley, 01/48/1.

[248] IWM: Mozley, 01/48/1.

attack, though no movement could be discerned at that long range. The tattoo of the guns made me realise the meaning of the word "drum fire". The noise made by the guns was extraordinary, and I tried to analyse it. The continuous bark of the guns seemed to resemble St Vitus-like arpeggios played, staccato, upon a gigantic piano, while the scream of the shells was like a devil's chorus far up in the scale.[249]

Despite being overcast the air forces of both sides were extremely active and when they were not being strafed from the air the infantry took an interest in what was going on above them. Captain Mozley wrote,

One morning there was a tremendous battle in the air between two groups of aircraft. One of our planes was separated somehow from the rest, and was shot down in flames near Le Transloy. The pilot made a gallant effort to get to ground, but without avail. The next day at almost the same spot a German machine crashed to the ground. We heard later that the pilot of the first plane was a Cambridge cricketing Blue. On another occasion, one of our artillery machines (spotter plane) was attacked by a German scout, which had twice its speed. In addition, the British plane was hampered by a strong Westerly wind, which tended to take it over the enemy lines. Just as things looked serious, a cascade of rockets suddenly appeared from the artillery plane, which so disconcerted the attacker, that it (ours) got away unscathed.[250]

One evening just before sunset, when the clouds blew away, Lieutenant-Colonel Fife noted that he "saw 61 of our aeroplanes & 25 of our and the French balloons up at one time."[251] Mozley witnessed another aerial encounter while they were in the front line. On this day the weather was uncharacteristically fine and good for flying and spotting,

Planes were active all day, especially German ones, some of which penetrated far behind our lines ... A solitary German scout was returning from a reconnaissance about midday, and our anti-aircraft

---

[249] IWM: Mozley, 01/48/1.
[250] IWM: Mozley, 01/48/1.
[251] Personal diary of Lieutenant-Colonel Fife.

batteries were plastering the sky all around him, when there was a dramatic intervention. Tearing along at tremendous speed, and ignoring the archies, one of our machines fell on to his tail out of the blue. There was a faint rattle high up, and the next thing that we knew was that the German plane was falling in flames. It crashed about a mile north of us. A faint crackling, caused by exploding M.G. ammunition, came to our ears, and sounded strangely like distant applause. One wing of the aeroplane had been broken clean off, when it started to fall, and this floated gracefully down to the ground, looking like a silvery leaf in the distance.[252]

As already noted the conditions and weather were atrocious. In such circumstances the men could not remain long in the line and the plan, according to Lieutenant Hoyte, was for tours to be reduced to forty-eight hours, with 24 hours in reserve, forty-eight in a camp, 24 hours in reserve and then forty-eight hours back in the line. Captain Mozley remembered with bitterness that this seemingly neat arrangement was not the case for his men, "the physical condition of the men was much lowered by exposure and the absence of proper food and a hot drink. 'B' Coy was relieved after 3 days in the line, but we had 4 days of it …"[253]

Relief was eagerly awaited. Mozley remembered being relieved from duty in the front line, it was not straightforward; nothing there ever was,

I was about to go, when Briggs, my orderly, told me that Private Budgeon, of No. 1 Platoon, was stuck fast in the trench and was unable to move. (The humour of his name of course struck me instantly). He was an undersized little chap, not much over 5ft in height, and the privations of this tour had affected his physique, though not his spirit. It was clearly impossible to leave him stuck in the mud, so Briggs and

---

252 IWM: Mozley, 01/48/1.
253 IWM: Mozley, 01/48/1.

I divided his rifle and kit between us, and hauled him with a great squelch out of the mud, and over the back of the trench.[254]

There began a long and uncomfortable journey out of the line for Briggs, Budgeon and Mozley. They had gone but a short way when a bullet tore through Mozley's waterproof and rattled his water bottle. They threw themselves into whatever cover they could find and after a short pause in holes the three of them got going again. Budgeon was in a bad way so Mozley and Briggs left the man with the troops in the support line and carried on towards the rear. Mozley was glad to hear that Budgeon was well looked after and sent to hospital.[255]

Mud was the implacable enemy of all of the soldiers in France and Flanders, they feared it as much as shot, shell and gas. Captain Rogerson wrote of this same sector in November 1916 when his battalion went into the line. Going up he could hear…

…the constantly reiterated shout of "Halt in front! Halt in front! Man stuck," as some poor devil sank to the waist in an unseen hole. I could feel the awful tenseness as the line waited till he had been hauled out.[256]

Often a man could not be hauled out and sank, drowning in the mud.

Shortly after leaving Budgeon, Mozley and Briggs realised that they were lost. By complete accident they bumped into their own No. 1 platoon. Still lost they did make their way towards a dim light but found a small group of men from another division that were as lost as they were. Mozley led his band off again and were shouted at by the men that they had just left. They were going towards the German lines and as if to prove this fact a flare soared into the darkness. Mozley and his men turned about face and headed back the way they had come. This time Mozley

---

254 IWM: Mozley, 01/48/1.
255 Private Herbert S. Budgeon was transferred from the 6th Dorsets to the Labour Corps and survived the war.
256 S. Rogerson, *Twelve Days on the Somme*, p. 33

decided to steer his band home by using the stars. It was a clear night and Mozley was able to recognise the Great Bear and the Pole Star. Keeping them on his right they trudged slowly and wearily towards the British rear. A solitary whizz-bang came their way but it plopped ineffectively into the mud nearby and failed to go off. Its miserable showing seemed to sum up the situation and everyone's mood. After a while they found their way back to the Sunken Road that led to Lesboeufs and their own HQ. From here they continued wearily on to Trones Wood camp.[257] So it went on as the battalions did their turns in the line and were then relieved. Up on the line, as Captain Mozley's lads settled down to rest, other battalions settled into the line for their tour.

---

[257] IWM: Mozley, 01/48/1.

The Capture of Zenith Trench

The centre of the 17th Division's section of the front line was held by one battalion of the 51st Brigade with one battalion in support. On the left was the 52nd Brigade and on the right the 50th. It was a 51st Brigade operation in early November that caught the attention of Fourth Army H.Q and brought about great praise and generated the short Reuters news report of 9 November. [258]

Moving up from the support positions to take over from the 10th Notts & Derbys, the 7th Borders were due to go into the front line on 1 November. Lieutenant-Colonel W. J. Woodstock[259] and his 2 i/c Major Reginald Strutt Irwin[260] of the 7th Borders went forward, with their company commanders on 31 October and observed the German front line, Zenith Trench. "Orders had already been issued [by 51st Brigade H.Q] to take Zenith Trench by surprise if it was at all possible."[261] So the officers set about assessing the situation. They studied Zenith Trench from

---

[258] The press was strictly controlled at this point in the war, a stark contrast to the early days of 1914/15 when the press had more freedom.

[259] Captain, temporary Lieutenant-Colonel, Woodstock of the Special Reserve had been in command of the 7th Borders for only eighteen days, he had arrived from the 9th Lancashire Fusiliers as a replacement for Lieutenant-Colonel Norrington on 13 September 1916. Woodcock did not return to the 7th Borders after recovering from his wounds but was sent instead to command a battalion of the Manchester Regiment. He was Mentioned in Despatches on 21 December 1917.

[260] Irwin had been a Captain when he joined the 7th Borders and was then promoted to temporary Major. He entered France and Flanders with the battalion on 15 July 1915. After a stint in command he left the 7th Borders and became the C.O. of the 3rd Black Watch with the rank of temporary Lieutenant-Colonel. He was awarded the D.S.O and Mentioned in Despatches on 25 May 1917, December 1917 and June 1918. After the war he transferred to the 2nd Black Watch and served with the British Army Of The Rhine.

[261] TNA: PRO. WO 95/2008. War Diary, 7th Borders, November 1916.

the right, the centre and the left of the British front line in this sector.[262] Woodstock and Irwin wanted to know, and they wanted their officers and men to know, exactly what and where they were planning to attack. It was known that Zenith Trench jutted out as a small salient towards the British front line called Misty Trench, faced that part of the British front line known as Gusty Trench and on the right it was even held by the British. The soldiers of both sides were only divided by stops manned by their respective bombers.

At dusk, while Lieutenant-Colonel Woodstock discussed the relief with officers of the 10th Notts & Derbys, a group of soldiers clearing up Needle Trench accidentally detonated a discarded explosive device. Nine men and the Colonel were wounded by shrapnel from the explosion. Woodstock's wounds were bad enough to need hospital attention and Major Irwin assumed command of the battalion. Later, before the relief began, four officers, second lieutenants Chafuniére,[263] Gordon R. Kyd, H. L. Morgan and Eddington, were sent forward to carry out single patrols to reconnoitre Zenith Trench, to find out where the 50th Brigade boundary was and to establish contact with that brigade.[264] They failed to bring back any useful intelligence. Therefore, when they went in to the line at the junction of Misty and Gusty Trenches on 1 November, the 7th Borders were already under orders to send out further patrols to find the exact location and dimensions of Zenith Trench.[265] It was a complicated objective and all possible intelligence was required.

---

262 Fourth Army Narrative, 9 November 1916 in TNA: PRO. WO 95/1981. War Diary, 17th Division, November 1916.

263 So far it has not been possible to identify this officer, or indeed discern if his name was spelled correctly in the 7th Border's war diary because when he is mentioned his name is spelt differently. Oddly, he only appears on 31 October and 1 November, there is no mention at all in the war diary of this second lieutenant before or after these dates. It is possible, with French units on the right of the 17th Division, that he was a French officer attached to the 51st Brigade.

264 TNA: PRO. WO 95/2008. War Diary, 7th Borders, November 1916.

265 TNA: PRO. WO 95/2008. War Diary, 7th Borders, November 1916.

The company taking over the front line, B Company, was commanded by a veteran officer, Captain Arthur Plater Nasmith.[266] B Company was understrength[267] and had in its ranks a number of new men who had recently arrived in a new draft, many of whom had never been 'over the top' before.[268] Relief of the line began at dusk[269] was completed by 10.45 pm and Captain Nasmith promptly sent four patrols out into the darkness, each with orders to locate Zenith Trench. Three were single 'officer patrols', Second Lieutenants Chafuniére, Kyd and Eddington and one was a larger patrol of three other ranks led by Second Lieutenant Morgan.[270]

These were the same four officers who had carried out patrols on the previous night and once again they had mixed fortunes as the darkness and ground conditions hampered their efforts.[271] Second Lieutenant Kyd returned with a German machine gun that he had found abandoned, though in good working condition, in a shell hole some 30 yards away from their own parapet.[272] He also produced two small books that he found on a dead German soldier that he came across in no-man's-land.[273] Second Lieutenant Eddington returned empty handed but with

266 Captain Nasmith had been with the 7th Borders since the formation and had been on the Western Front since the 17th Division came out from Britain. He had been Mentioned in Despatches on 15 June 1916. He was awarded the D.S.O for the Zenith Trench operation and was again Mentioned in Despatches on 22 June 1917 for his work during the Battle of Arras. By then he had been posted missing, in fact Nasmith had been killed in action on 23 April 1917 during the ill-fated attacks upon Bayonet and Rifle Trenches in the resumption of the Battle of Arras. His body was never recovered or identified.

267 Fourth Army Narrative, 9 November 1916 in TNA: PRO. WO 95/1981. War Diary, 17th Division, November 1916.

268 The last significant draft, 169 men, had arrived at the battalion on 27 September 1916. There had been no offensive action since then because the Gommecourt Front had been so quiet.

269 TNA: PRO. WO 95/2008. War Diary, 10th Notts & Derbys, November 1916.

270 TNA: PRO. WO 95/2008. War Diary, 7th Borders, November 1916.

271 TNA: PRO. WO 95/2008. War Diary, 7th Borders, November 1916.

272 TNA: PRO. WO 95/2008. War Diary, 7th Borders, November 1916. The basis for the Reuters news story.

273 TNA: PRO. WO 95/1981. War Diary, Daily Intelligence Summary, 17th Division, November 1916.

the news that he could not find any sign on the 50th Brigade on the right of Gusty Trench. No contact, therefore, could yet be made with the troops on the right. That would be vital. If the attack was to go ahead, the 50th Brigade would have to know about it. It appears that Second Lieutenant Chafuniére returned with no news or intelligence at all and Second Lieutenant Morgan and his three men simply did not return. No news of Second Lieutenant Morgan and his patrol could be got and Captain Nasmith and B Company had no clearer information about Zenith Trench. Ironically Morgan and his men had been too successful, they found Zenith Trench alright, and they walked straight into it and the hands of the German garrison. Morgan was wounded, probably shot by a sentry, and the four men were captured.[274] Time was ticking on and morning was approaching.

Not satisfied with the poor intelligence returned by these patrols Captain Nasmith sent out two further officer patrols to locate Zenith Trench.[275] This time they found it,

> One reported that he found the junction of Eclipse – Zenith and the left of Zenith to be fairly strongly held, judging from the talking and whistling. No wire could be seen. The ground leading up to Zenith was in exceedingly bad condition owing to the heavy shelling. His work was interfered with by our artillery shelling the junction of Eclipse and Zenith during the progress of his patrol. No Very lights were sent up from Zenith but many appeared to come from a short distance behind. Progress was very slow, owing to the amount of dead lying in shell holes and the churned state of the ground.[276]

The other officer reported that he approached Zenith Trench from the centre and that he heard men working in the trench and patting down earth. Captain Nasmith concluded that Zenith

---

274 TNA: PRO. WO 95/2008. War Diary, German Prisoner's report post the first part of the Zenith Trench Operation, 7th Borders, November 1916.

275 TNA: PRO. WO 95/2008. War Diary, 7th Borders, November 1916.

276 TNA: PRO. WO 95/1981. War Diary, Daily Intelligence Summary, 17th Division, November 1916.

Trench itself was not strongly held.[277]   By the time the last officer returned at 4.00 am, the plans to take a trench, about which the attackers still knew little, had been tentatively laid but daylight was breaking and the attack could not go ahead. Information about the trench itself might have been hazy but they did have an idea which units they faced. Elements of the 15th Bavarian Reserve (Bavarian Ersatz) Division were holding the German line.[278]   It was also believed that the 15th Bavarian Reserve Infantry Regiment and the 28th Ersatz Regiment were also in the sector having both been identified from documents brought in by patrols and prisoners.[279]   Despite the uncertain intelligence, in the early hours of 2 November Captain Nasmith and Major Irwin signalled their plans and willingness to attack in the early evening of 2 November to 51st Brigade H.Q. Preparations for the operation went ahead as Irwin and Nasmith waited for Brigade to reply.

Written orders were issued and the 10th West Yorks on the right and the 9th Northumberland Fusiliers on the left were warned. During the morning 2 Lt Sanger was sent to the right of Zenith Trench then in the occupation of a company of the 7th Lincolns, and made arrangements that if the attack was a success three Very lights would be fired in rapid succession from the right enemy bombing stop [in the German held part of Zenith Trench[280]] to close into the left …[281]

Although it is not recorded in the 51st Brigade war diary, permission to carry out the operation was granted by Brigadier-General Trotter at 2 pm on 2 November.[282] Therefore, Major

277 TNA: PRO. WO 95/2008. War Diary, 7th Borders, November 1916.

278 Miles, *Official History, 1916, Vol II*, p. 469.

279 TNA: PRO. WO 95/1981. War Diary, Daily Intelligence Summary, 17th Division, November 1916.

280 Part of Zenith Trench was held by the 7th Lincolns on the right and they had a bombing stop set up in the trench on their left. The Germans also had a bombing stop set up so there was a gap in the trench between the two stops that it was hoped the 7th Lincolns, on seeing the red Very Lights would rush and take.

281 TNA: PRO. WO 95/2008. War Diary, 7th Borders, November 1916.

282 TNA: PRO. WO 95/2008. War Diary, 7th Borders, November 1916.

Irwin and Captain Nasmith set the time of attack for dusk; between 5.30 and 6.00 pm. B Company would mount the attack, supported by the battalion bombers under Second Lieutenant Edward Sanger,[283] three Lewis Gun teams and one platoon of D Company. Captain Nasmith would lead the attack with four other officers and the force totalled some 129 men.[284] It was to be "a direct frontal attack, consisting of about 70 bayonets, with bombers and Lewis Guns on each flank."[285] There would be no preliminary bombardment by the artillery, only the usual night time firing.[286]

The attack was planned for dusk (5.30 pm), on 2nd November. At this hour the company that carried out the attack was situated in the southern part of Misty Trench and the northern part of Gusty Trench. The whole company got out of the trench and worked its way to a line parallel to the position of Zenith Trench to be attacked and awaited orders. It took half an hour to get the company into line. When everything was ready for the attack to be launched the whole company crawled forward...[287]

The 7th Borders own war diary continued,

The attack started at 6 pm and was a complete success. In the dim moonlight our men got in on the left without being observed and got within 20 yards on the right without observation. The left was taken without much opposition but a sharp bombing attack ensued on the right in which some 20 to 30 enemy were killed. The Lincolns on the right refused to believe that the trench had been taken and [instead of

---

283 Edward Sanger later earned the M.C., and was promoted to lieutenant. He survived the war.

284 TNA: PRO. WO 95/2008. War Diary, 7th Borders, November 1916.

285 51st Brigade Narrative, 8 November 1916 in TNA: PRO. WO 95/1981. War Diary, 17th Division, November 1916.

286 Fourth Army Narrative, 9 November 1916 in TNA: PRO. WO 95/1981. War Diary, 17th Division, November 1916. This would ensure surprise because a bombardment would have alerted the defenders and it would also save time because the attackers would not have to wait for an artillery programme to be drawn up.

287 Fourth Army Narrative, 9 November 1916 in TNA: PRO. WO 95/1981. War Diary, 17th Division, November 1916.

rushing the gap] opened rapid fire and also bombed. The gap therefore between the bombing stops could not be taken [and a small garrison of German infantry was left in possession of a portion of the trench between the Borders and the Lincolns]. Zenith Trench was at once consolidated and advance patrols sent out. A post was established in Eclipse Trench (a trench heading back towards the enemy) about 150 yards towards the enemy.[288]

As soon as it was signalled that Zenith Trench had been taken the,

… left company (7th Border Regiment), which was occupying the northern part of Misty Trench, went forward and commenced to dig a trench (the present Blizzard Trench) from the junction of Eclipse and Zenith Trenches to a point in Misty Trench.[289]

Connection was soon made between the trenches. The operation had been a success and the good news was soon reported back to a delighted Brigade staff. A search of the newly captured portion of trench revealed that twenty-five German soldiers had died along with Second Lieutenant W. Jackson[290] and Lance Corporal Frederick Arthur Hart.[291] Eight Borders' had been wounded. Apart from the failure to clear the gap out, and the Borders blamed the Lincolns for that, it had been a remarkable little victory. For a time the German troops in the gap remained behind their bombing stops and were initially very quiet and the German artillery for once failed to fire on their captured position. The British surmised that the German gunners were uncertain about the situation and held their fire for fear of hitting their own men. This state of affairs did not last for long and,

---

[288] TNA: PRO. WO 95/2008. War Diary, 7th Borders, November 1916.

[289] Fourth Army Narrative, 9 November 1916 in TNA: PRO. WO 95/1981. War Diary, 17th Division, November 1916.

[290] Jackson is recorded in *Soldiers Died in the Great War* as Arthur Jackson.

[291] Hart is recorded by *Soldiers Died in the Great War* as being killed on 3 November 1916 but is the only other rank of the 7th Borders killed in action on 2 or 3 November 1916.

...at 8 p.m. [British] artillery night lines were lengthened 200 yards beyond Zenith Trench and 50 yards up Eclipse Trench, and the rate of artillery fire increased. A strong barrage was put down by the enemy, from time to time, on Rainbow Trench and a less severe barrage on Misty and Gusty Trenches.[292]

At 11.00 pm the 7th Borders were relieved in Misty, Gusty and Zenith Trenches by the 7th Lincolns.[293] Of the operation on 2 November the 7th Lincolns said nothing, instead their war diary for 2 November recorded, "Relieved 7th Border Regt in front line. Disposition, four companies in front line. Bn H.Q. in Sunken Road. Usual heavy shelling and sniping."[294] Nonetheless, they were about to play their part in the battle for Zenith Trench because it was by no means all over. Now that the operation had been successful 51st Brigade got in on the act and became involved in the planning for the capture of the gap and for further operations against the German trenches. First of all the German infantry made attempts to regain Zenith Trench.

At dawn, about 6.30 am, on 3 November, a German counter-attack developed on Misty, Gusty and Zenith Trenches from some old gun pits to the east of Eclipse Trench. The German troops were spotted by the Lincolns and were allowed to come to within 75 yards of Zenith before the Lewis guns and rifles opened fire. The attack was decimated in no-man's-land and the Lincolns, who estimated that attacking force to be about 200 men, noted that over 100 had been killed and four German soldiers were captured.[295]

---

[292] Fourth Army Narrative, 9 November 1916 in TNA: PRO. WO 95/1981. War Diary, 17th Division, November 1916.

[293] Fourth Army Narrative, 9 November 1916 in TNA: PRO. WO 95/1981. War Diary, 17th Division, November 1916.

[294] TNA: PRO. WO 95/2007. War Diary, 7th Lincolns, November 1916.

[295] TNA: PRO. WO 95/2007. War Diary, 7th Lincolns, November 1916. & Fourth Army Narrative, 9 November 1916 in TNA: PRO. WO 95/1981. War Diary, 17th Division, November 1916.

Half an hour later some 80 German soldiers were seen to stand up in no-man's-land and made signs that they wished to surrender. The 7th Lincolns company commander in the nearest trench signalled them to come in to the British lines but as he did so someone on the right opened fire and killed one of the surrendering German soldiers. Unsurprisingly the German soldiers took cover once more in no-man's-land and throughout the day some of these men tried to make it back to their lines; as they did so the Lincolns shot them down.[296]   A very similar incident was recorded by 51st Brigade H.Q., as happening at 11.00 am that morning but it is so similar that it is likely to be the same event. The only difference in the story, apart from the time, was that once the German troops took cover they began to snipe at the Lincolns.[297]   Of this incident or incidents, the 7th Lincolns recorded nothing.

Between 3.00 and 4.00 pm a serious German infantry counter-attack developed against the British line and it began with a bombardment of the British trenches and barrages were also laid down. At first three waves of German infantry advanced from the direction of a German trench known as Beam Lane. Using the same tactic as earlier in the day the 7th Lincolns allowed the first two waves to come within about 100 yards before the Lewis guns and rifles opened fire. Once again, the leading waves were shot down in no-man's-land. Artillery support was called for and the third wave advanced into an artillery barrage and was cut to pieces. British reports of this action stated that very few of the estimated 200 German soldiers who took part in this suicidal frontal assault survived to get back to their own lines. A further group of German troops attacked the bombing stop in Eclipse Trench and succeeded in capturing it after it was hit by shells sometime around 4.00 pm. Fighting with the men out in no-

---

[296]   Fourth Army Narrative, 9 November 1916 in TNA: PRO. WO 95/1981. War Diary, 17th Division, November 1916.

[297]   51st Brigade Narrative, 8 November 1916 in TNA: PRO. WO 95/1981. War Diary, 17th Division, November 1916.

man's-land continued until about 6.00 pm but the fight for the bombing stop in Eclipse Trench went on.[298]

By now the 7th Lincolns had gone on the offensive against the German garrison in the gap in Zenith Trench. They had wanted to bomb the part of the trench held by German troops as soon as possible but did not have enough bombs to do the job. This news reached Lieutenant-Colonel Fife, CO of the 7th Yorks, the Green Howards, 50th Brigade, in the front line nearby. He sent a bombing squad, under the command of his bombing officer, Lieutenant Watt and his deputy Sergeant William Hornby[299] with extra bombs and orders to co-operate with the 7th Lincolns in any way they could.[300]

With this extra help from the 7th Yorks, as sporadic fighting was still going on, the 7th Lincolns "seized the opportunity of clearing up the situation at the E. end of Zenith Trench."[301] Between 5.00 and 6.00 pm, as darkness fell,[302] A Company led by Captain R. Pennington and the bombers under Lieutenants J. R Williams and Watt of the 7th Yorks climbed out of their part of Zenith Trench and worked their way through no-man's-land behind the German held gap.[303] Once they were in position the Lincolns and Yorks rushed the gap from the surface.[304] The 51st Brigade narrative recorded,

They arrived to find the Germans looking towards Misty Trench; they threw their bombs and charged into and along the top of the trench. A

---

[298] Fourth Army Narrative, 9 November 1916 in TNA: PRO. WO 95/1981. War Diary, 17th Division, November 1916. & 51st Brigade Narrative, 8 November 1916 in TNA: PRO. WO 95/1981. War Diary, 17th Division, November 1916.

[299] Hornby was later awarded the M.M. and survived the war.

[300] Personal Diary of Lieutenant-Colonel Fife.

[301] Fourth Army Narrative, 9 November 1916 in TNA: PRO. WO 95/1981. War Diary, 17th Division, November 1916.

[302] Personal Diary of Lieutenant-Colonel Fife.

[303] TNA: PRO. WO 95/2007. War Diary, 7th Lincolns, November 1916. It is worth mentioning that the 7th Lincolns war diary makes no mention of the assistance rendered by the 7th Yorks.

[304] Fourth Army Narrative, 9 November 1916 in TNA: PRO. WO 95/1981. War Diary, 17th Division, November 1916.

German got his machine gun up and turned it round to fire; before he could do so Lieut. Williams put his revolver to his neck and killed him, no doubt by his promptness saving many lives. During this fight, several Germans held up their hands, at the same time throwing a grenade, which may account for the number of them killed here, viz. 48. The bombers took 38 prisoners in this trench; the casualties of this bombing party were two slightly wounded. No further attack was attempted by the enemy during the night 3/4th. and the work of consolidation proceeded without hindrance...[305]

Lieutenant-Colonel Fife added that four machine guns were captured and that Lieutenant Watt had been wounded in the face;[306] the 7th Lincolns recorded that two German officers were also taken prisoner.[307]

It had been a very satisfactory episode in the battle for Zenith Trench. Fighting still carried on but died down as the evening progressed and it took until 8.20 pm to recapture and re-consolidate the bombing post in Eclipse Trench. It was only then that, "The officer commanding 'B' Company, 2nd Lieut. Thomas, 7th Lincolnshire Regt., ... was able to report all gains held."[308]

Fourth Army noted that for the whole operation, "The enemy's total casualties were estimated at 360, ours at 5 officers and 75 other ranks." [309] The 7th Lincolns remained in the line and consolidated the trenches. Their casualties were recorded as, Second Lieutenant J. E. Robinson and 24 Other Ranks killed and Second Lieutenant R. H. Merryweather and 70 Other Ranks wounded. Ten Other Ranks were missing.[310] The battalion was

---

[305] 51st Brigade Narrative, 8 November 1916 in TNA: PRO. WO 95/1981. War Diary, 17th Division, November 1916.

[306] Personal Diary of Lieutenant-Colonel Fife.

[307] TNA: PRO. WO 95/2007. War Diary, 7th Lincolns, November 1916.

[308] 51st Brigade Narrative, 8 November 1916 in TNA: PRO. WO 95/1981. War Diary, 17th Division, November 1916.

[309] Fourth Army Narrative, 9 November 1916 in TNA: PRO. WO 95/1981. War Diary, 17th Division, November 1916.

[310] TNA: PRO. WO 95/2007. War Diary, 7th Lincolns, November 1916.

relieved on 4 November.[311] Zenith Trench had been securely added to the British front line opposite Le Transloy.

News of the complete capture of Zenith Trench soon filtered up to the Fourth Army staff and they were very happy. Once the reports were gathered together at Fourth Army H.Q. a narrative of the operations was compiled. General Rawlinson was so pleased with the efforts of the 17th Division men that he had the narrative published and on 9 November distributed throughout his army as an exemplar of good infantry work. It demonstrated, "good leading by officers and, the fine fighting spirit shown by all ranks."[312]

While the story remained largely the same, to serve certain encouragement and training purposes the story was altered slightly in a couple of areas. The rather confused and unsuccessful patrols that failed to even find the trench and that had to be sent out again and again were recorded by Fourth Army as, "four patrols were sent out to make a thorough reconnaissance of the ground that had to be crossed."[313] No mention was made of the patrol that got captured. Interestingly the, "sharp bombing attack on the right"[314] made by the 7th Borders on 2 November during the initial attack became "Heavy bayonet fighting," in the Fourth Army Narrative.[315] There was a feeling in some higher circles of the British Army that the infantry were placing too much reliance upon the Mills bomb grenade and not relying enough upon the good old 'cold steel' of the bayonet. While the narrative implied that there had been co-operation between two battalions this had not really been the case.   The 7th Borders had begun the job and by not co-

311 TNA: PRO. WO 95/2007. War Diary, 7th Lincolns, November 1916.
312 Fourth Army Narrative, 9 November 1916 in TNA: PRO. WO 95/1981. War Diary, 17th Division, November 1916.
313 Fourth Army Narrative, 9 November 1916 in TNA: PRO. WO 95/1981. War Diary, 17th Division, November 1916.
314 TNA: PRO. WO 95/2008. War Diary, 7th Borders, November 1916.
315 Fourth Army Narrative, 9 November 1916 in TNA: PRO. WO 95/1981. War Diary, 17th Division, November 1916.

operating properly as per the plan on 2 November, the 7th Lincolns left themselves with the job of completing the capture of the trench on the following day. Which they did but, as has been seen, with a higher loss of life than the 7th Borders on 2 November. Fourth Army's description of Zenith and Eclipse Trenches was, however, accurate and made the capture of Zenith Trench all the more remarkable.

The condition of Zenith and Eclipse Trenches was indescribable. Part of Zenith Trench itself was merely a series of craters joined by a ditch knee deep in water. In many parts of the trench it was absolutely impassable, being waist deep in water.[316]

There is no denying the achievement of the capture and consolidation of Zenith Trench but it does speak volumes for the realistic expectations and objectives of the Somme Campaign in November 1916. The great plans and hoped for sweeping advances of the summer months had become, at Le Transloy at least, truly bogged down in the increasingly colder Picardy mud.[317]

The successful operations that captured Zenith Trench impressed the generals from brigade level, on through Division, Corps and up to Fourth Army. Quite apart from the fact that the battle for Zenith was a victory it was in the first instance conceived at brigade level[318] and then planned, ordered and executed at battalion level.[319] Such initiative, such offensive spirit by the infantry in such awful conditions in a campaign that had been dragging on for months pleased the generals greatly.

---

[316] Fourth Army Narrative, 9 November 1916 in TNA: PRO. WO 95/1981. War Diary, 17th Division, November 1916.

[317] The Reserve Army operating north of the Albert – Bapaume Road on firmer ground and with fewer supply issues did manage to take Beaumont Hamel and the Thiepval – Ginchy Ridge on 13 November but the Somme Campaign was by then coming to a halt of its own accord.

[318] TNA: PRO. WO 95/2008. War Diary, 7th Borders, November 1916.

[319] Fourth Army Narrative, 9 November 1916 in TNA: PRO. WO 95/1981. War Diary, 17th Division, November 1916. & 17th Division Narrative in TNA: PRO. WO 95/1981. War Diary, 17th Division, November 1916.

The Somme's End

There were other operations besides those at Zenith. On 3 November the 52nd Brigade mounted a tiny operation against a German Strong Point opposite Mild Trench. As part of a larger operation, Finch and Orion Trenches were attacked by Battle Patrols of the 50th Brigade on 5 November. In none of these operations, for the 17th Division, was the success at Zenith Trench replicated. The men were tired, dragged down by the gruelling conditions which were, as has been seen, appalling. The exhaustion that gripped the divisions of the Fourth Army was not going un-noticed at high level, the generals *did* keep a watchful eye on their troops. The XIV Corps commander was one such general.

Lord Cavan was concerned and unimpressed by the Fourth Army's orders for his Corps to attack German positions on 5 November. The strength of the German defences, the mounting casualties, the morale of his men and the growing difficulty of going onto the attack all occupied his mind. On 3 November he wrote to General Rawlinson, saying,

> *With a full and complete sense of my responsibility, I feel it my bounden duty to put in writing my carefully considered opinion as to the attack ordered to take place on November 5th. I have previously said that in my opinion the only way to attack Le Transloy is from the south and to this I adhere. An advance … from my present position with the troops at my disposal has practically no chance of success, on account of the heavy enfilade fire of concealed machine guns and artillery from the north, and the enormous distance we have to advance against a strongly prepared position, owing to the failures to advance our line in the recent operations.*

My Corps has already lost 5,320 men in attacks ... I perfectly acknowledge the necessity of not leaving the French left in the air, but I would point out that when the French find an impossible trench in front of them they do not attempt it ...

I assert my readiness to sacrifice the British right rather than jeopardise the French success, but I feel bound to ask if this is the intention, for a sacrifice it must be. It does not appear that a failure can much assist the French and there is a danger of this attack shaking the confidence of the men and officers in their commanders. No one who has not visited the front trenches can really know the state of exhaustion to which the men are reduced.[320]

The attacks by the 17th and 33rd Divisions went ahead, they could very well not do.

During the course of the 17th Division's tour, apart from providing covering fire during the Zenith Trench operation, the 52nd Brigade mounted only one operation. This was the tiny attack against a German Strong Point at 5.00 pm on 3 November. The brigade's war diary entry reads that at 11.30 am,

The 10th Lancashire Fusiliers were ordered to attack a German Strong Point at 5.00 pm. The Lancashire Fusiliers report attack failed to reach objective, owing to heavy hostile machine gun fire and shrapnel barrage.

The Strong Point proved to be much stronger than anticipated. The ground was in such a bad condition that the men were exhausted before they had covered many yards, also the trenches were, in most place, waist deep in liquid mud and after 24 hours the men became unfit for offensive operations. This, therefore, did not allow sufficient time for a careful reconnaissance of the enemy's position.[321]

---

[320] Lieutenant-General, the Earl Cavan in TNA: PRO. WO 95/911. War Diary, XIV Corps, November, 1916.

[321] TNA: PRO. WO95/2006. War Diary, 52nd Brigade, November 1916.

The 10th Lancashire Fusiliers' diary for the day had little to add about the episode.[322] The battalion had taken over the front line trench of the 52nd Brigade sector, Mild Trench, from the 9th Duke of Wellingtons on the previous day, 2 November. The Strong Point was situated on the right front of Mild Trench and was attacked by two bombing squads supported, presumably with covering fire, by two platoons. As 52nd Brigade recorded, the attack was a failure and the Germans responded by attacking a bombing stop set up on the left of Mild Trench, held by the 10th Lancashire Fusiliers. This German attack was beaten off and a number of men were killed during the day including Second Lieutenant George Hoskins and R.S.M., Goulding.[323] For the rest of the tour the 52nd Brigade consolidated and held the line. In fact the brigade's battalion war diaries are uninformative for this time (unlike the detailed accounts made by all 17th Division battalions earlier in the Somme Campaign or the more informative diaries kept by the 50th and 51st Brigade battalions in November and December), containing only mundane comments about units moving here and there. This brigade was holding the line rather than going on the offensive like the 50th and 51st Brigades.

The 50th Brigade made more concerted attacks but not in large numbers, such as the 7th Yorks' Battle Patrol Attack upon Finch Trench and the 7th East Yorks' attack on Orion Trench on 5 November 1916.[324] The 7th Yorks were to attack, capture and consolidate Finch Trench, the German front line opposite Zenith Trench. On Brigadier-General Glasgow's orders Lieutenant-Colonel Fife was limited to attack the objective with only 40 riflemen and bombers because larger scale attacks were to be made on both the left and right flanks of the 7th Yorks.

---

322 TNA: PRO. WO95/2012. War Diary, 10th Lancashire Fusiliers, November 1916.

323 The Commonwealth War Graves Commission and *Soldiers Died in the Great War* record different death dates for these men. Hoskins, 5 November and Goulding, 4 November. However, the war diary states that they were killed on 3 November.

324 TNA: PRO. WO 95/2004. War Diary, 7th Yorks, November 1916. & Lieutenant-Colonel Fife's Personal Diary.

There would be a preliminary bombardment of the objective. 'A' Company would provide the Battle Patrol and they would advance from the British front line, Zenith Trench, over the open, in two lines with a bombing squad on each flank. Every man in the second line had to carry a shovel to enable the patrol to consolidate the objective once it was taken. Captain Lewis Wilberforce Goldsmith would lead the attack assisted by Second Lieutenant S. J. House and Captain S. B. Kay would be in overall command in Zenith Trench. One officer and an N.C.O. were tasked with keeping touch with the 7th East Yorks attacking Orion Trench on the right. The 20th Royal Fusiliers of 19th Brigade, 33rd Division who would attack on their right.[325]

The Battle Patrol was to be covered by a battery of 6-inch guns of the heavy artillery and the guns of the divisional artillery covering the 17th Division. Lewis guns of A and B Companies and heavy machine guns would also be in position to cover the assault; all machine gun crews were under orders not to open fire unless the enemy did. A battery of Trench mortars would also be on hand to bombard Finch Trench. Once the objective was taken and consolidated it would be held by Lewis gun teams. The captured trenches were to be connected to the British line by communication trenches. During the night before the attack patrols were to be sent out to make sure that the shell holes between the British front line and the objective were clear of German troops. Orders and arrangements for the 7th East Yorks' Battle Patrol against Orion Trench were practically the same, other than that Battle Patrol was larger by 20 men.[326]

They would be operating against objectives that they could not see or recognise. Just like the Zenith Trench operation before, these trenches bore little or no resemblance to the trenches used and attacked earlier in the campaign and could be difficult to

---

[325] TNA: PRO. WO 95/1981. War Diary, 17th Division, November 1916. & TNA: PRO. WO 95/2004. War Diary, 7th Yorks, November 1916.
[326] TNA: PRO. WO 95/1981. War Diary, 17th Division, November 1916. & TNA: PRO. WO 95/2004. War Diary, 7th Yorks, November 1916.

locate among the shell holes and undulating ground. With this in mind 50th Brigade Operation Order No. 112 contained the advice, "Assaulting troops are to be warned that they may have difficulty in recognising the objectives as trenches on reaching them, and should know beforehand what distance they had to go [to the objective]."[327]

On the night of 4/5 November officer patrols duly went out and confirmed that the shell holes between the lines were empty.[328] Grenades arrived at 9.30 am and Lieutenant-Colonel Fife made sure that his bombers had plenty.[329] At 10.00 am on 5 November the preliminary bombardment fell on and around Finch Trench heralding the beginning of the operation. While Fife said, "Very heavy bombardments began about 10.00 am, gradually intensifying to barrage by our guns on enemy front line."[330] Major-General Robertson was dubious about the effectiveness of the bombardment and wrote,

The nearness of Finch Trench to Zenith and the great difficulty of getting men back ready to attack if withdrawn for the preliminary bombardment prevented the barrage being put on the trench, although an attempt to shell it was made before zero hour.[331]

The Trench Mortar Battery failed to show up. Not that it mattered noted Lieutenant-Colonel Fife, because "I don't think that they could possibly have been used in the present state of the ground."[332]

At 11.10 am, and in broad daylight, the Battle Patrols of both the 7th Yorks and 7th East Yorks left Zenith Trench and, following a creeping barrage that lifted every 25 yards, advanced upon Finch and Orion Trenches. Observers reported that the

327 TNA: PRO. WO 95/2002. War Diary, 7th East Yorks, November 1916.
328 TNA: PRO. WO 95/2004. War Diary, 7th Yorks, November 1916.
329 Lieutenant-Colonel Fife's Personal Diary.
330 Lieutenant-Colonel Fife's Personal Diary.
331 Major-General Robertson in TNA: PRO. WO 95/1981. War Diary, 17th Division, November 1916.
332 Lieutenant-Colonel Fife's Personal Diary.

German garrison was seen running in large numbers away from Finch Trench as the 7th Yorks' Battle Patrol moved forward. That state of affairs did not last long because someone looked back towards the Battle Patrol and, "seeing how small our assaulting party was, they halted and opened fire on them."[333] Captain Goldsmith was hit and wounded as was the other officer, Second Lieutenant House. With both officers down the attack slowed and the men took cover in the shell holes. They tried to go forward, hurling bombs as they did so but if any men reached Finch Trench they were either killed or captured. By 2.30 pm the attack was over.[334] Lieutenant-Colonel Fife later wrote in his brief report about the action,

> *Report by O.C. 7th Yorks Regt. Finch Trench (name given to objective for convenience in reporting) was attacked by my battle patrol at 10 a.m. yesterday. The trench was rather strongly held. The enemy probably outnumbered my men. The attack was repelled chiefly with rifle fire.*[335]

The 7th Yorks' Battle Patrol had failed before it reached Finch Trench.

Initially it was a different story for the 7th East Yorks in their part of the operation. At 11.10 am, under the command of Second Lieutenants Frederick William Drew and Cyril Bisdee Major, "They moved forward behind a good barrage & in such excellent spirits that all men were smoking as they went over. They reached Orion with not more than 3 casualties & the enemy were seen leaving the trench in great numbers..."[336] But it was the last that was heard of most of the Battle Patrol. At 12.02 pm Captain Douglas Foster Grierson, in command of the 7th East Yorks operation from Zenith Trench, sent twelve men out from

---

[333] TNA: PRO. WO 95/2004. War Diary, 7th Yorks, November 1916.

[334] TNA: PRO. WO 95/2004. War Diary, 7th Yorks, November 1916. & Lieutenant-Colonel Fife's Personal Diary. & TNA: PRO. WO 95/2002. War Diary, 7th East Yorks, November 1916.

[335] TNA: PRO. WO 95/1981. War Diary, 17th Division, November 1916.

[336] TNA: PRO. WO 95/2002. War Diary, 7th East Yorks, November 1916.

Zenith Trench to Orion as reinforcements, even though none had been called for, and he also despatched two runners with orders to gather information about the situation in Orion Trench and to report back.

At 12.20 Captain Grierson reported to battalion H.Q. that the Battle Patrol had gained the objective and he had received no signal that they required reinforcements.[337]   Major King, commanding the 7th East Yorks since Lieutenant-Colonel Clive had been wounded, wrote,

> *Report by the O.C. 7th E. Yorks Regt. We attacked at 11.10 a.m. with 2 officers and 60 men, viz, 40 rifles and 20 battalion bombers. They got over under the barrage with very few casualties.[338]*

However, beyond this there was no news of the Battle Patrol nor any messages from them.   Captain Grierson's runners returned, wounded, at around 12.25 and reported that they could not get across to Orion so they could not reach the Battle Patrol. They did say that the German troops were no longer retiring from their positions but were counter attacking and bombing. Still they waited for news but none was forthcoming from Orion.   By 2.45 pm news had reached Grierson that the 20th Royals Fusiliers on his right and the 7th Yorks on his left had been held up and that their attacks had failed to gain the objectives.[339]

Nonetheless, even at that point with the attacks on both flanks failed and with no evidence to back up his belief, Major King wrote that he was "certain that we were still holding Orion."[340] At 4.30 pm he sent D Company under Captain J. Moore to relieve B & C Companies in the front line but shortly afterwards Moore reappeared at King's battalion H.Q., suffering from Shell

---

[337] TNA: PRO. WO 95/2002. War Diary, 7th East Yorks, November 1916.
[338] TNA: PRO. WO 95/1981. War Diary, 17th Division, November 1916.
[339] TNA: PRO. WO 95/2002. War Diary, 7th East Yorks, November 1916.
[340] TNA: PRO. WO 95/2002. War Diary, 7th East Yorks, November 1916.

Shock.[341] D Company had been left under the command of Second Lieutenant Metcalf.[342]

Captain Grierson was trying to make his way to battalion H.Q. when, at 7.30 pm, he was shot and wounded by a sniper.[343] Command of the Orion Trench operation now devolved to Captain Calvert and his first act was to send out a patrol of six men under Sergeant John E. Wragg[344] to finally ascertain what was actually going on in Orion Trench. Only Wragg and one man returned alive to report that they had found Second Lieutenant Drew's body in no-man's-land, got to within 20 yards of Orion and had been close enough to see that it was occupied by German soldiers. It seems that the other five men of Wragg's patrol had paid for this information with their lives. As Wragg reported to Calvert, as if to back up his report, a number of Very Lights were fired from Orion Trench over Zenith. At 9.20 pm Calvert was able to report to Major King something that should have been obvious to the officers for hours; Orion Trench had not been held by the Battle Patrol.[345] What had happened to the 7th East Yorks' Battle Patrol has not been recorded but the clue must be in the report made by the two runners sent out at 12.02 pm by Captain Grierson; they said that the Germans were counter attacking and bombing. These German troops must have fought back and regained control of their trench.

Incredibly, for the whole afternoon it seemed to the 7th Yorks and to those at 50th Brigade H.Q. that all was going well. At 12 noon Lieutenant-Colonel Fife, suffering from headache, neuralgia, wet feet and in an overcrowded, tiny and unhealthy

---

[341] Moore was fit for service again five days later.

[342] TNA: PRO. WO 95/2002. War Diary, 7th East Yorks, November 1916.

[343] It took three hours for the medics to get him away from Zenith Trench and back to medical help. Grierson's signal book and paperwork are to this day stained with his blood. According to his medal index card he relinquished his commission before the war's end on 10 January 1918 and in 1922 was living on the Kalumpang Estate, Malaysia.

[344] John E. Wragg who rose to the rank of W.O. II and was discharged before the war ended.

[345] TNA: PRO. WO 95/2002. War Diary, 7th East Yorks, November 1916.

H.Q. dug-out, had received a report from the O.C. 7th East Yorks saying that his Battle Patrol had achieved its objectives and that the enemy were "running like hell".[346] Then, at 12.50 pm, Lieutenant-Colonel Fife received a heartening report from Lieutenant Robertson of A Company stating that he *thought* that the 7th Yorks had gained their objective but one of the patrol officers, Captain Goldsmith, had been wounded. Realising that things might not be a good as they sounded Fife warned Captain Bartrum's D Company to prepare to send two of their three platoons forward to Zenith Trench in order to support the Battle Patrol or, if the attack had failed, to launch another assault on Finch. Fife also sent out an orderly to Zenith Trench with orders for Captain Kay to report his situation.[347]

The German artillery was by now busy shelling the British trenches and the German riflemen were alert. In Zenith Trench Captain Kay and Second Lieutenant Reginald Theodore Rudge had both been hit by shell fire. Twenty-four year old Kay[348] had been wounded and Rudge killed. Second Lieutenant C. I. Eyre was also wounded, shot in the hand. Captain Goldsmith, found in no-man's-land by medics searching for casualties,[349] was shot dead on his stretcher along with three of the bearers trying to rescue him.[350] The 7th Yorks were running out of officers in the front line.

D Company's platoons under Captain Bartrum were in place at Zenith Trench by dusk and at some point between 5.45 pm and 8.00 pm the 7th Yorks discovered from Captain Thomas

---

346 Lieutenant-Colonel Fife's personal diary.

347 TNA: PRO. WO 95/2004. War Diary, 7th Yorks, November 1916. & Lieutenant-Colonel Fife's personal diary.

348 Captain S. B. Kay recovered from his wounds and transferred to the Royal Flying Corps. He was wounded again and sent to hospital in Leeds where he died of his wounds in 1918.

349 These men were probably battalion stretcher bearers. No R.A.M.C. men were killed in action on the Western Front on 5 November 1916 and none of the division's Field Ambulances record any bearer losses.

350 TNA: PRO. WO 95/2004. War Diary, 7th Yorks, November 1916. & Lieutenant-Colonel Fife's personal diary.

Huffington, despatched by Lieutenant-Colonel Fife to gather information, that their Battle Patrol had failed to capture Finch and that Captain Goldsmith was dead.[351] The situation on the right in Orion Trench was still obscure at this time. However, in Zenith Trench, Bartrum reported that his two platoons would attack Finch Trench at 10.00 pm under cover of darkness and that they would try to surprise the German garrison by crawling towards the objective. This information was passed up the chain of command to 50th Brigade H.Q., who passed it on to 17th Division, who passed it on to XIV Corps who at 9.50 pm sent orders cancelling Bartrum's attack.[352] They did not want the attack to go ahead until it was clear that the 7th East Yorks had taken Orion Trench on the right.[353] Time had been wasted, the cancellation orders arrived too late and at 10.00 pm the two platoons under the command of Lieutenant H. P. Gregory and Second Lieutenant A. C. Goodall climbed out of Zenith Trench and crawled through the mud, dead bodies and shell holes of no-man's-land towards Finch Trench, in an attempt to take the German defenders by surprise.[354]

It did not take the alert Germans in Finch Trench long to detect the approaching British and they opened fire with rifles and machine guns. Gregory and Goodall were among the first hit, Gregory was wounded and Goodall was killed. The attack, no stronger than the one in the morning, was dealt with in similar fashion by the German defenders and failed in the mud of no-man's-land.[355] It later became clear that the 7th East Yorks had

---

[351] Lieutenant-Colonel Fife's diary and the battalion war diary are at odds over the time of this discovery.

[352] It is rather surprising that Corps would concern themselves over platoon level attacks.

[353] TNA: PRO. WO 95/1998. War Diary, 50th Brigade, November 1916. & TNA: PRO. WO 95/2004. War Diary, 7th Yorks, November 1916. & Lieutenant-Colonel Fife's personal diary.

[354] TNA: PRO. WO 95/2004. War Diary, 7th Yorks, November 1916. & Lieutenant-Colonel Fife's personal diary.

[355] TNA: PRO. WO 95/2004. War Diary, 7th Yorks, November 1916.

failed as well and no more attacks against Finch Trench were launched by the 7th Yorks.

It had not been a strong battalion in terms of numbers when it had gone into the line and now the 7th Yorks were in a sorry state. Losses in the war diary were recorded as three officers killed and five wounded, twenty-seven other ranks killed, 70 wounded and ten missing. A Company had practically ceased to exist; B Company had one officer, Second Lieutenant H. Collins, left; C Company had spent the entire day carrying supplies forward and D Company only had one intact platoon.[356] They were exhausted and those left alive were in a bad way thanks to the conditions and the strain of shelling and combat. Relief could not come soon enough and that came the following day.[357]

It was a similar story for the 7th East Yorks. The battalion had not been strong and had gone into the line with sixteen officers and 560 other ranks. The war diary recorded that one officer had been killed, five wounded and one was missing. Eighteen other ranks had been killed, 84 wounded and 84 were missing. These figures were later revised up. Two officers, Second Lieutenants Drew and Major, and 47 Other Ranks had been killed.[358] Not inconsiderable casualties for such an operation.

All that the 10th Notts & Derbys recorded about 5 November, as they stood in the support positions was that, "The Hun unconsciously celebrated Guy Fawkes Day by putting up the most extraordinary number of coloured Very Lights without any apparent reason."[359] Focussed on their job of supporting the 8th South Staffords in the line in front of them it appears that the 10th Notts & Derbys had no idea that attacks were going on nearby. Such was the nature of these small operations by companies, platoons and sections to capture portions of ill-

---

[356] TNA: PRO. WO 95/2004. War Diary, 7th Yorks, November 1916.

[357] TNA: PRO. WO 95/2004. War Diary, 7th Yorks, November 1916.

[358] TNA: PRO. WO 95/2002. War Diary, 7th East Yorks, November 1916. & *Soldiers Died in the Great War.*

[359] Hoyte, *10th (S) Battalion* p. 23.

defined trenches and a few shell holes. A day later the 10th Notts & Derbys were similarly involved themselves and Lieutenant Hoyte's words echo the opinion of the British Army at this point in the Somme Campaign and sum up the victory at Zenith Trench,

> *Capt. T. W. Daniel, with a small party of men, drove the enemy out of some old gunpits about 80 yards from our front line; the pits were then linked up to our trench. During the following night a bombing party advanced about 350 yards eastwards along Eclipse Trench with little resistance; a stop was established, and a trench was then dug running north-eastwards from the stop to our front line. These advances, though small, denied observation to the enemy, and were made in such appalling conditions that they were really very fine performances.*[360]

Two men of the 10th Notts & Derbys were killed in action on 6 November but it is not known if they died in Captain Daniel's successful little venture.

So, the Battle for Zenith Trench was the last successful battle for the 17th Division on the Somme in 1916 and the words "No event of importance to record" [361] appeared regularly in the divisional war diary from 5 November onwards. Sniping, patrolling, working parties and shelling went on along the front but operations by the 17th Division to add more German trenches to the British front line had ceased. Notice for the relief by the Guards Division was given on 8 November, on 9 November the Narrative of the successful operation at Zenith Trench was distributed throughout the Fourth Army. The irrepressible Lieutenant Eric Boyce was wounded on 9 November and it was the start of a long series of operations, he lost an arm but was still keen to get back into the war.[362] Orders

[360] Hoyte, *10th (S) Battalion* p. 23

[361] TNA: PRO. WO 95/1981. War Diary, 17th Division, November 1916.

[362] TNA: PRO WO 95/2000. War Diary, 6th Dorsets, November 1916. & O' Hanlon, *A Plain History of the Sixth (Service) Battalion*, p. 123

for the relief by the Guards on 14 November arrived on 10 November. To quote the history,

> *After this [the 5 November operation] till the Division was relieved by the Guards on November 14th, there were no important events, but only the daily and nightly round of service in the muddy trenches, with occasional skirmishes between patrols.*[363]

For some battalions in the division there were none of these successful ventures, no matter how small. The 10th West Yorks, for instance, were struggling on. On 9 November sickness and casualties had dramatically reduced the battalion in numbers and all available rear echelon men were put into the line to reinforce the fighting companies. The war diary for 10 November recorded, "the majority of the men were greatly exhausted."[364] On the following day, "There were many cases of Trench Feet and Captain S. B. E. Cutler[365] and 39 sick men were evacuated to hospital direct from A Camp."[366] They were not the only battalion suffering like this. The 9th Northumberland Fusiliers[367] noted that on 10 November "The Colonel [G. P. Westmacott] went straight from the trenches to the hospital and Capt Allen took over the Com'd of the btn."[368] Even though actual Trench Foot figures were not recorded in the war diaries at the time, the

---

363 Atteridge, *History of the 17th (Northern) Division*, p. 175

364 TNA: PRO. WO 95/2004. War Diary, 10th West Yorks, November 1916.

365 Captain Seymour Bernard Egston Cutler had been on the Western Front since the 17th Division began to arrive there on 13 July 1915. He did not return to the West Yorks but was sent instead to the Labour Corps. In December 1918 he was serving at the Labour Corps Record Office, 13 Carrington Street, Nottingham. The Labour Corps Record Office was a large concern commanded by Lieutenant-Colonel Reginald Frederick Myles Formby and employed a large staff. Many of these were women and this caused serious trouble after the war's end when demobbed soldiers wanted the girls sacked so that they could have their jobs. This building once stood where, until very recently, the Broadmarsh Bus Station stood, on a tatty and grubby fragment of Carrington Street.

366 TNA: PRO. WO 95/2004. War Diary, 10th West Yorks, November 1916.

367 TNA: PRO. WO 95/2013. War Diary, 9th Northumberland Fusiliers, November & December 1916.

368 TNA: PRO. WO 95/2013. War Diary, 9th Northumberland Fusiliers, November 1916.

instances of Trench Foot and sickness in certain battalions could not be kept from Brigade or Division and there would be a price to pay.

The difficulties of the conditions and the situation were continuing to cause disquiet among the generals of all grades and not being blind to the suffering that the troops were enduring, they were genuinely concerned for their men. Major-General Robertson visited some of his division just after they left the line and their pitiful state moved him to write in his (now lost) diary,

> *We went to see the W. Yorks just in from the trenches; they are in an awful state, only 200 able to walk; a very large number of cases of frost-bite on both hands and feet. This last fortnight has undoubtedly been the most trying of the war. The weather conditions have been simply appalling and the trenches awful – men buried in mud for two or three days at a time before they could be dug out – several deaths from exposure alone – cases even of men drowned in the mud. The men have borne it splendidly in spite of all – with no hot food or fires and very little drinking water. I wonder if those behind the lines have the slightest conception of what it is like.*[369]

General Rawlinson had taken heed of General Cavan's words of 3 November and knew them to be true and he was well aware of how his corps and divisional generals felt. He wrote to Sir Douglas Haig, "General Rawlinson had written to the Commander-in-Chief on the 7th November to point out that his battle-weary divisions required rest and were all in urgent need of the opportunity to assimilate new drafts and to train for future operations."[370]

If anyone thinks that the High Command were unaware of the conditions on the Somme or the suffering of the troops they are wrong. On 21 November Sir Douglas Haig wrote,

---

[369] Major-General P. R. Robertson in Atteridge, *History of the 17th (Northern) Division*, p. 174

[370] Miles, *Official History, 1916, Vol II*, p. 535.

The ground, sodden with rain and broken up everywhere by innumerable shell-holes, can only be described as a morass, almost bottomless in places : between the lines and for many thousands of yards behind them it is almost – and in some localities, quite – impassable. The supply of food and ammunition is carried out with the greatest of difficulty and immense labour, and the men are so much worn out by this and by the maintenance and construction of trenches...[371]

Reverend Duncan wrote,

Haig felt keenly the losses and the sufferings of the men in the trenches. He did not speak much about this. But no one who knew him had any doubts that he was deeply and personally concerned. Now and then his deeper feelings would come to the surface. For example, in a letter to Lady Haig in April 1917, he confessed to 'a tremendous affection for those fine fellows who are ready to give their lives for the Old Country at any moment'; and added: 'I feel quite sad at times when I see them march past me, knowing as I do how many must pay the full penalty before we can have peace.' This sense of sadness was never far absent...[372]

Major-General G. P. T. Feilding of the Guards Division took over the line at 10.00 am on 14 November from Major-General Robertson and the 17th Division travelled by units, by train and in convoy to Treux. Captain Mozley remembered that journey and wrote that on a misty morning they marched away from the Somme battlefield and on to Edgehill Station at Dernancourt where they were put on trains and sent to Hangest, beyond Amiens. Each train was made up of 42 Third Class carriages, two First Class carriages, two flat trucks and two brake vans.[373]

---

[371] Sir Douglas Haig's report to C.I.G.S., 21 November 1916 in Miles, *Official History, 1916, Vol II,* p. 536.

[372] G. S. Duncan, *Douglas Haig As I Knew Him,* (George Allen and Unwin Ltd, First published, 1966), p. 49

[373] TNA: PRO. WO 95/2005. War Diary, 51st Brigade, November 1916.

These were fairly long trains but it has to be remembered that the carriages of the day were not large.[374]

Mozley's troop train stopped at Amiens Station and he remembered that, "there was the usual frantic scene at Amiens Buffet,"[375] as soldiers scrambled to get refreshments. The trains then went on to Hangest where lorries met them and took the troops to the rest area at Molliens en Vidame. Mozley did not go with them, he parted company at Amiens and went on leave, his first since February.[376]

On 14 November Major-General Robertson issued orders to his men for their training. While they were to train in the full range of infantry arts, attention was to be given to Close Order Drill and musketry. As his men marched and rode to the rest area Major-General Robertson requested the loan of three drill sergeants from the Guards Division and three bayonet

---

[374] By November 1916, at the request of the French rail authorities, who up to this time had provided all of the rolling stock and the 409 mainline locomotives to haul them, some British locomotives and rolling stock had begun to arrive on the Western Front. However, these trains operating out of Edgehill were more than likely of French composition. The question of railway operation and the use of locomotives, rolling stock and crewing were difficult subjects for both the British and French authorities. At the beginning of the war the French had demanded that they handle all railway traffic, apart from any shunting that the B.E.F. required, and the British, as junior partners in 1914, agreed but it was a decision that, by late 1915 and early 1916, they came to regret. By November 1916 there was a growing shortage of railway stock in France and much of what was in traffic was wearing out (as were the metals on which the trains ran). Some American engines were on order by the British for service in France and some South Eastern tank engines were already shunting at the channel ports. There were some Belgian locomotives but they were either too light, too heavy, in need of an overhaul or simply missing. (Many trains had fled over the border into France when the Germans over ran Belgium, and a number had been absorbed into the French Railways). In November 1916 the British were happy to run their own railway affairs in France and Flanders and sent an initial batch of 300 locomotives, their crews and a large number of rolling stock out to the Western Front. For further information see A. M. Henniker, *Transportation On The Western Front*, (First published, H.M.S.O, 1933. Re-printed Imperial War Museum and Naval & Military Press, 2009) & Pratt, Edwin A, *British Railways and The Great War, Organisation, Efforts, Difficulties and Achievements*, Vol I & II, (London, Selwyn and Blount, Ltd, 1921).

[375] IWM: Mozley, 01/48/1.
[376] IWM: Mozley, 01/48/1.

instructors from Fourth Army. Frost bite, trench foot and exhaustion notwithstanding, there would be no slacking in the rest area; the division had to train up to be effective once more. On 16 November divisional H.Q was established at Cavillon and that training commenced.[377]

The 7th Borders[378] noted that on 9 November a British aircraft was brought down in no-man's-land. The observer was killed but the pilot, Lieutenant Cowie of 11 Squadron was brought into the Borders' trench. He was wounded in his foot.[379]

Rest Billets and Personnel Issues

The units began to arrive in the rest billets in the Cavillon area on 15 and 16 November. Despite the increasing cold and rain showers which became snow and regular mist and fog, training began almost as soon as the units arrived and the billets were allocated. Even though the formation was out of the line the business of running and managing the division and the units within it carried on as normal. There was some serious personnel business to attend to because some senior posts were on the line.

Brigadier-General Glasgow visited Lieutenant-Colonel Fife on 17 November, "who told me that he is expecting to go home, being considered too old for his job."[380] On 20 November Brigadier-General Clarke handed the 52nd Brigade over to Brigadier-General Godfrey Davenport Goodman,[381] and

---

377 TNA: PRO. WO 95/1981. War Diary, 17th Division, November 1916.
378 TNA: PRO. WO 95/2008. War Diary, 7th Borders, November & December 1916.
379 TNA: PRO. WO 95/2008. War Diary, 7th Borders, November 1916.
380 Personal Diary of Lieutenant-Colonel Fife.
381 Brigadier-General Godfrey Davenport Goodman, C.M.G., D.S.O., V.D. Had originally been a reserve captain and was soon promoted to major in the Territorial Force. He became Lieutenant-Colonel of the 1/6th Notts & Derbys and went out to the Western Front with that battalion on 12 February 1915. After serving as the temporary commander of 52nd Brigade he moved on to command

proceeded to Britain on a secondment.[382] Goodman himself had been given little notice of his promotion and had left Gapennes to take over that very day,[383] and as for Clarke the only reason given for his replacement was that he, "… had now completed two years' service in France."[384] However, compared to the Zenith Trench success of the 51st Brigade, Clarke's brigade had achieved nothing on the Somme in November 1916. On taking command of 52nd Brigade Brigadier-General Goodman became a very busy man and from the end of November onwards he was a regular visitor at his four battalions.[385]

It would appear that Brigadier-General Glasgow was indeed under scrutiny from Major-General Robertson because of the health of his brigade. Therefore, he began to consider two of his battalion commanders' futures for allowing Trench Foot to take hold and it did not take him long to act. Three days later, on 20 November, Lieutenant-Colonel Fife invited Brigadier-General Glasgow to visit his battalion to inspect a new draft of men from Britain whom Fife considered "a poor lot." There was a change in Glasgow's mood and Fife later wrote that the Brigadier-General seemed "more cheerful and I fancy has been reprieved."[386] It would seem that Glasgow had acted decisively because later that day Fife had another visitor at his billet; it was Lieutenant-Colonel Soames. "Soames, commanding W. Yorks

the 21st Brigade. He was Mentioned in Despatches on, 1 January 1916, 15 June 1916, 15 May 1917, 20 May 1918 and 20 December 1918.

[382] Atteridge, *The History of the 17th (Northern) Division*, p. 174 – 5. However, his post at the 52nd Brigade was not held open as one might imagine. On his return to the Western Front in February 1917 he was given the prestigious command of the 3rd Brigade in the 1st Division. He then requested a transfer back to the 17th Division which was granted in March 1917. His second term in command of the 52nd Brigade was cut very short by an illness that appears to have finished his career as a brigade G.O.C., but not as a soldier. His Medal Index Card shows that he had a staff job in Afghanistan in 1919.

[383] TNA: PRO. WO 95/2694. War Diary, 1/6th Notts & Derbys, December 1916.

[384] Atteridge, *The History of the 17th (Northern) Division*, p. 174

[385] TNA: PRO. WO 95/2013. War Diary, 9th Northumberland Fusiliers, November 1916.

[386] Personal Diary of Lieutenant-Colonel Fife.

came to tell me that he has been "Stellenbosched"[387] on account of number of trench feet in his Battn."[388] Only in command since 26 July 1916, he was to pay the price for his battalion's Trench Foot epidemic and general poor physical health by losing his command and the rank of Lieutenant-Colonel. Glasgow did not stop at Soames and to the fury of the officers of the 6th Dorsets he dismissed Lieutenant-Colonel Rowley. On 22 November Lieutenant-Colonel Fife wrote, "Met Rowley, commanding the Dorsets, who told me that he too is being sent home for the same reason as Soames." [389]

Brigade H.Q took a direct hand in the running of the 10th West Yorks and they probably did the same with the 6th Dorsets, (although that battalion did not record any staff interference but then it did not record the trench foot epidemic either). "Under direction from Brigade Headquarters the early morning physical training parades were stopped."[390] The men of the 10th West Yorks were deemed not fit enough for their 'physical jerks'. Musketry and general company training aplenty was ordered and Brigadier-General Glasgow himself visited the battalion on 24 November to see how things were going. It must have been galling for Soames, who was still present and nominally in command to be side-lined in this manner by his Brigadier-General. The following day Divisional H.Q. got involved with the 10th West Yorks and made certain that, "Under Divisional Instructions FOOT FRICTION DRILL is to commence morning and afternoon."[391]

---

387 To be Stellenbosched was to be sent away from one's unit in disgrace and denied promotion. The term came from the Boer War when officers deemed incompetent were sent to the town of Stellenbosch. While retaining their ranks they were employed to look after horses. In effect they were sent away to a place where they could do no harm to their own side.

388 Personal Diary of Lieutenant-Colonel Fife.

389 Personal Diary of Lieutenant-Colonel Fife.

390 TNA: PRO. WO 95/2004. War Diary, 10th West Yorks, November 1916.

391 TNA: PRO. WO 95/2004. War Diary, 10th West Yorks, November 1916.

The 50th Brigade had certainly been shaken up. Of the 50th Brigade battalion commanders, with Clive wounded and never to return, Soames and Rowley dismissed in disgrace, only Fife remained. Although, if Brigadier-General Glasgow thought that 'Stellenbosching' two of his battalion commanders was going to save his job he was mistaken. On 30 November, confident of his position, he put in a request for leave to Divisional H. Q., starting 3 December; the request was refused.[392]

In stark contrast Lieutenant-Colonel Fife visited Major-General Robertson, bypassing Brigadier-General Glasgow with whom he had obviously had no joy in terms of his poor drafts, to complain about, "130 'Bantams' I am anxious to get rid of…"[393] and to protest at having the 50-year-old Captain J. R. Stone,[394] who had arrived with a draft of 50 men,[395] in his battalion. Fife, who was only 48, thought Stone too old for the trenches… What Major-General Robertson said on the subject of the 'Bantams' or Stone was not recorded but, "to my astonishment the General told me that he intended to recommend me for a month's leave. Doubt whether I shall get it."[396] But he *did* get leave and he was even given a car and driver to take him to Amiens Station to begin that leave on 2 December.[397] Fife was popular with the divisional commander and was possibly in line to be promoted to Brigadier-General.[398]

As for Brigadier-General Glasgow, he was swiftly dismissed within days of asking for leave and he handed command of the 50th Brigade over to Brigadier-General C. Yatman, D.S.O., on 3 December.[399] No reason was given in the 17th Divisional

392 Personal Diary of Lieutenant-Colonel Fife.
393 Personal Diary of Lieutenant-Colonel Fife.
394 Formerly of the King's Own Yorkshire Light Infantry.
395 TNA: PRO. WO 95/2004. War Diary, 7th Yorks, November 1916.
396 Personal Diary of Lieutenant-Colonel Fife.
397 Personal Diary of Lieutenant-Colonel Fife.
398 Preface to the Personal Diary of Lieutenant-Colonel Fife.
399 TNA: PRO. WO 95/2004. War Diary, 7th Yorks, December, 1916.

History for his removal,[400] but in reality it was the scourge of Trench Foot; that and the 50th Brigade's lack of success on the Somme in November 1916. Glasgow never held a combat command again, instead he took up a training post in Britain with the new and growing Tank Corps.[401] His career's end had more dignity than Soames' or Rowley's..

On 11 December[402] Soames handed command over to Major P. R. Simner[403] the C.O. of the 9th Duke of Wellingtons, West Riding Regiment; who in turn left Major. S. Danby in command of his battalion.[404] On 13 December the C.O., of the 6th Dorsets, Lieutenant-Colonel Rowley, who had commanded since the formation of the battalion in Dorset in 1914, was recorded as going on leave,[405] and "Major G. B. de Mairis, the [1st] Yorkshire Regiment, succeeded, fresh from India."[406] Captain O'Hanlon wrote of Rowley,

---

[400] Atteridge, *The History of the 17th (Northern) Division*, p. 174

[401] Medal Index Card.

[402] TNA: PRO. WO 95/2004. War Diary, 10th West Yorks, December 1916.

[403] Percy Reginald Owen Abel Simner had gone to the Western Front with the 9th Duke of Wellington's, West Riding Regiment as a temporary captain on 15 July 1915. He was promoted to major and then to Lieutenant-Colonel when he took over the 10th West Yorks. He was awarded the D.S.O and Mentioned in Despatches on 15 June 1916, 4 January 1917 and 18 December 1917. Simner had commanded the 9th Duke of Wellington's with distinction and he had helped to make the unit an excellent battalion, possibly the best in the 52nd Brigade. If anyone could turn the 10th West Yorks around he could and he did. Simner survived the war.

[404] TNA: PRO. WO 95/2014. War Diary, 9th Duke of Wellingtons, West Riding Regiment, December 1916.

[405] TNA: PRO. WO 95/2000. War Diary, 6th Dorsets, November & December 1916.

[406] He arrived on the Western Front in 1916 and was posted to the 7th Yorks; when Rowley's job came up he was posted to command the 6th Dorsets. He then moved on to command the 2nd West Yorks, made a permanent Lieutenant-Colonel instead of a temporary one (meaning that he would keep that rank at the end of the war instead of reverting to a previous permanent rank) and was awarded the D.S.O. Mairis survived the war. At the time when he took over the 6th Dorsets he was a 'rookie' in terms of the Western Front and that can be seen in O'Hanlon and Mozley's writings. He may have been regular army but the veterans treated him with a certain amount of disdain.

The bitter loss to the Battalion was the departure of Lieut.-Colonel Rowley. He had fathered and patiently trained it from the first day; his first thought was for its good name and for the welfare of the men. He commanded it far longer than any of his successors; he had led it into the trenches and into its first battles. After the fashion of early days the Battalion might have been called 'Rowley's'...[407]

Captain Mozley also wrote about Rowley's dismissal and like O'Hanlon he refused to cite the reason for the colonel's removal,

The news that the C.O. was leaving us had reached us at Molliens. As I am hopelessly biased, I can say nothing on the subject of his removal, but I should imagine that the Brigadier's ears must have burned during the month of December and for some time afterwards.[408]

Glasgow probably did not 'give a jot' about Rowley's dismissal. The latter returned to Britain and joined the home based 3rd Battalion with the rank of major. The 3rd Battalion's main purpose was to send new drafts out to the fighting battalions. When Soames left the 10th West Yorks he was not sent home but instead returned to his original unit, the 1st West Yorks in the quiet sector at Cambrin and like Rowley he reverted to the rank of major. Twenty-four days later Soames was Mentioned in Despatches but less than a month after leaving the 10th West Yorks, on a very quiet day at Cambrin, with no offensive operations on-going and very little in the way of artillery and sniper fire, he died; the only casualty of the day.[409]

---

[407] O' Hanlon, *A Plain History of the Sixth (Service) Battalion*, p. 125-6

[408] IWM: Mozley, 01/48/1.

[409] It took Soames four days to reach his old battalion and he arrived at Cambrin on 15 December. His Mention in Despatches was noted in the 1st Battalion diary on 5 January 1917. Then on 9 January 1917, *'Trenches. Quiet day. Major G. G. Gilligan assumed command of the battalion. Casualties – killed, Major G. H. Soames."* He was the first fatal casualty of the New Year and only the sixth since 11 December 1916. There was not another fatal casualty until 17 January 1917 and after that only five more men were killed up to the end of the month. Cambrin was a very quiet sector. Soames was recorded on the WW 1 Service Medal and Award Rolls as a Lieutenant-Colonel when his widow received his medals in 1920. TNA: PRO.

Administration, Training, Rest and Recreation

For the lower ranks, both officers and men, their days were given over to work, rest and occasionally play; the doings of the generals went often on beyond their ken. As usual the working day began with physical exercise and then military training followed, which was very much the same as earlier in the year: musketry, drill, map reading. Then platoon, company, battalion and brigade schemes, route marching, night marches by compass, bayonet fighting and specialist training with Lewis Guns and bombs.

Divisional H.Q. concerned itself with a range of administrative matters and the paperwork was generated to advise, instruct and order. Major-General Robertson wanted a division that went by the book and was regimental, probably because he believed that a smart division was an efficient division. Censorship was an issue. "The Censorship of letters, including those of Junior Officers, to be looked into. The writing of pessimistic letters as regards to the local situation in France being against orders." March discipline (one of Major-General Robertson's favourite subjects), particularly that of the cooks, and their lack of cleanliness was a matter arising. New officers had to be trained to oversee the digging of trench systems. Drill Instructors and Gym Instructors were to be banned from going into the front line; they were only to go into the line if "a shortage of N.C.Os occurs." The Major-General was keen on his close-order drill so this matter arose from the fear that their skills would be lost should they be killed and the men would not be able to drill properly. Saluting was slack within the division and needed to be smarted up. Too many pieces of furniture were being stolen or smashed up (probably for fire wood) in the billets so inventories would be issued listing the items in each billet. It

WO95/1618. War Diary, 1st West Yorks, December 1916 & January 1917. & WW 1 Service Medal and Award Rolls.

had been seen that the men were sloppy in the hut camps and billets therefore barrack room discipline would be enforced. Kit would be neatly folded and officers would inspect billets on a regular basis. Grease would be issued for the trenches and whale oil in the camps, but Division failed to mention what this was for even though it was, and is obvious: the dreaded Trench Foot. The division had to provide 50 officer candidates per month but there was some concern about the age limit for these men, the fear of compulsion, worry about expense and the problems caused by large numbers of senior N.C.Os leaving the battalions for commissions. These issues would therefore be brought up at Corps level. Khaki grenade badges were to be issued to company bombers. The list went on.[410]

In the evenings conferences were held and lectures given. For instance, Major-General Robertson let it be known that he wanted the junior officers to be thoroughly trained in the theory and practice of patrolling and how to obtain the best results from patrols. The notes about reconnaissance and preparation, normal patrols,[411] special patrols[412] and, contact patrols,[413] attention to detail, what kit to take and speed of reporting, among other points sent out to the brigades by division were to be used "as a basis for a lecture" by battalion or company commanders. Each brigade had ten copies of the notes; two for each battalion plus two spare sets on which the officers could base their lectures.[414] The Specialists took their turn in the lecture theatres as well, for instance the C.R.E., was down to give a series of two lectures at the Divisional School at Daours.[415]

---

410 TNA: PRO. WO 95/1981. War Diary, 17th Division, December 1916.
411 For regular information gathering, checking wire, listening posts and the domination of no-man's-land.
412 Patrols with a specific objective, usually small patrols carried out by expert scouts.
413 To keep in touch with the enemy after an attack, so as to know where the enemy is.
414 TNA: PRO. WO 95/1981. War Diary, 17th Division, December 1916.
415 TNA: PRO. WO 95/1990. War Diary, C.R.E., December 1916.

General, the Earl, Cavan also visited to give talks, and proved himself to be a popular officer and speaker.[416] Lieutenant Hoyte wrote that Cavan, "seemed to be, more than any other General of similar rank, so thoroughly human and appreciative of the point of view of the poor wretch in the front line."[417] Cavan did like making speeches and could certainly get the crowd going; Captain C. P. Blacker of the Coldstream Guards recalled,

> ... *a speech delivered by Lord Cavan, the Corps Commander, from inside the ring before the boxing began. It was about the essential importance of the bayonet. This heavily decorated officer told with relish some bouncing stories about how various units had used the bayonet ... The speech was vigorously delivered with semi-jocular conviction and went down well.*[418]

Captain Charles Carrington of the 1/5th Royal Warwicks had a slightly different angle on the Corps Commander and later noted that Cavan was, "an exponent of rigid defence and cramming the front line with troops. Cavan was a tough fighting soldier, and a charming man, but as the official historian [Brigadier-General Edmonds] wrote to me, 'bone from the neck up.'"[419] Perhaps, but his lectures and talks would have brought some levity to the regular training programme and seemed to have been a cross between instruction and entertainment. Cavan probably knew this and was not, perhaps, as 'thick' as Edmonds opined.

Even in rest the lethal nature of the war was never far away and being out of the line and in training still held its dangers. A note in the 7th Borders' *Summary of Casualties, December 1916* said that Second Lieutenant J. W. Simpson had been killed in an accident on 9 December.[420] No further details were given and the

---

416 Personal Diary of Lieutenant-Colonel Fife.

417 Hoyte, *10th (S) Battalion*, p. 24.

418 Blacker & Blacker (ed), *Have you Forgotten Yet?*, p. 172

419 C. Carrington, *Soldier From The Wars Returning*, (First published, Hutchinson & Co, 1965. Republished, Pen & Sword 2006 & 2015), p. 226.

420 TNA: PRO. WO 95/2008. War Diary, 7th Borders, December 1916.

incident was not recorded in the main text of the war diary, but John Watt Simpson from the Isle of Skye was not a green young soldier. He had been a Kitchener Volunteer and gone out to the Western Front as Rifleman Simpson, B3213, in the 8th Rifle Brigade on 20 May 1915.[421] Selected to become an officer he had been commissioned into the 7th Borders on 6 November 1916. His arrival at the battalion was not recorded but barely a month[422] after being commissioned he was killed in an accident.[423] A clue to the cause of his death may lie in the 8th South Staffords war diary. On 8 December it says, "Trench mortar accident at School of Mortars, Lt F. H. Cotterell of 8 S. Staffords severely wounded."[424] Given that all other records state that Simpson died on 8 December it is possible that he was on a trench mortar course at the school with Cotterell when the accident occurred. Simpson was not with the battalion long enough to leave an impression; a fate shared by so many.

It was not all hard work and training for the officers and men, Lieutenant-Colonel Nicholson and his quartermaster staff tried to make sure that there were diversions and entertainment for the troops. Football was popular and the fixtures and leagues were overseen and administered by the Adjutant & Quartermaster's branch.[425] Similarly, the divisional theatrical

---

[421] Notably, the 8th Rifle Brigade, 41st Brigade, 14th Light Division, suffered over 400 casualties taking Switch Trench during the Somme Campaign on 15 September 1916.

[422] There is a discrepancy over the date of his death, the war diary records it as 9 December, the Medal Index Card as 8 December, the WW 1 Service Medal and Award Rolls as 8 December and the Commonwealth War Graves Commission as 8 December.

[423] The WW 1 Service Medal and Award Rolls record that his medals were cancelled and his name has been crossed off the list but that was only because the medal issue was duplicated. His medals were all issued as an officer not as a Rifleman.

[424] TNA: PRO. W O 95/2007. War Diary, 8th South Staffords, December 1916. Frederic Hampson Cotterell had first come out to the Western Front when he joined the 8th South Staffords on 19 October 1916. He died of his wounds at Amiens on 16 December 1916 and was buried on the following day. Simpson is buried near Amiens.

[425] TNA: PRO. WO 95/1986. War Diary, Assistant Adjutant and Quarter Master General, 17th Division, December 1916.

troupe, "The Duds", were sent around the battalions, along with the mobile cinema, with orders from the Quartermaster to give performances in whichever suitable buildings they could find. [426] Amiens was near and offered shops and civilisation. There were cafés, bars and restaurants in the area where, if they had the funds, officers and men alike could get a meal and drink that had not been provided by an army canteen. [427] Lieutenant-Colonel Nicholson also made certain that the huge pile of dirty washing was dealt with and a divisional laundry under the A.S.C., was finally set up in Amiens to tackle the job. [428]

In a break from the routine some men were loaned to local farms to pull turnips. [429] Happily, there were baths and the men could get clean and stay clean and slowly the men began to smarten up. There was some sombre work for the 10th Notts & Derbys to do however. On 24 November the war diary of the A.D.M.S., recorded that on 25 November, Medical Officer Captain John Samuel Levis[430] would to attend the execution at Cavillon of veteran soldier Private William Henry Randle,[431] 10th Notts & Derbys for desertion. [432] The execution was duly carried out at

[426] O' Hanlon, *A Plain History of the Sixth (Service) Battalion*, p. 125. & TNA: PRO. WO 95/1986. War Diary, Assistant Adjutant and Quarter Master General, 17th Division, December 1916.

[427] Personal Diary of Lieutenant-Colonel Fife.

[428] TNA: PRO. WO 95/1986. War Diary, Assistant Adjutant and Quarter Master General, 17th Division, December 1916.

[429] Personal Diary of Lieutenant-Colonel Fife.

[430] Levis went out to the Western Front prior to December 1915 as a lieutenant in the R.A.M.C. He was a major by the war's end.

[431] Private Randle had been a Kitchener Volunteer and had served at Gallipoli with the 9th Notts & Derbys before being sent to the 10th Battalion. His Medal Index Card records, "shot for desertion". Randle had been born on Wollaton Street, Hucknall before he and his family moved to Shirebrook. William was a miner before joining up. His name was not originally on the Hucknall War Memorial but my friend and colleague, the historian Jim Grundy, fought successfully to have his name included on the town's Memorial.

[432] TNA: PRO. WO 95/1989. War Diary, A.D.M.S., November 1916.

dawn on 25 November; the firing squad would have been provided by the 10th Battalion.[433]

In December, as Christmas and a return to the line approached, a choice of what to do for Christmas was left to the individual battalions, there were no hard and fast rules or orders concerning the celebration. The 10th Notts & Derbys chose to have their Christmas Day out of the line on 10 December. The 10th Battalion's Christmas dinner was locally purchased pork washed down with beer and the men were given the afternoon and evening off to digest both. In the evening the officers dined in the Mess and the alcohol flowed; it was, wrote Lieutenant Hoyte "a very cheery show."[434] Other units chose to celebrate Christmas on different days and Captain Mozley recalled that,

> *On Dec. 20th the Christmas dinner was issued to the men. It consisted of pork, ham and vegetables, with some fruit. A turkey had arrived for me from home, and we had a most excellent repast on the same day, which was shared by some S. Staffs officers who were relieving us.[435]*

While there was some training for units other than those with a combat role, they continued to carry out their roles. For the Vets in the Mobile Section based at Oissy there was plenty to do as sick and lame animals were brought to them from a variety of units. There was no mention in the diary of Christmas festivities of any sort, rather the impression was of relentless, ceaseless work as the animals came in, were treated and either returned, retained or evacuated. While the division was in rest Captain Keppel, the C.O., and senior veterinarian in the 29th Section, fell ill and was forced to take sick leave. He was ill for a month and

---

[433] Unsurprisingly the battalion did not record this event. There is a good deal of information to be found on the internet about the men who were 'shot at dawn'.

[434] Hoyte, *10th (S) Battalion*, p. 23.

[435] IWM: Mozley, 01/48/1.

returned to his unit on 6 January 1917.[436] The loss of one Vet would increase the burden of work for the others in the Section.

The men of the 34th Sanitary Section continued to look after the sanitary requirements of the division while it rested and trained. They also carried out the "erection of several public latrines, public urinals and other useful structures in Corbie," when the division went into Corps reserve. On their return to the line they took over the forward baths and sanitation for the division.[437] Their work carried on as normal and without pause.

Illnesses such as chills, Influenza, dysentery and the dreaded Trench Foot were rife and continued to send men to hospital.[438] Yet the medics in the 51st and 52nd Field Ambulances noted that it was a quiet time. Life dealing with sickness cases would have brought its own challenges but without the flow of battle casualties, without gas, gunshot, blast and shell wounds it would have seemed like a holiday. However, there was a need to increase the capacity to deal with the increasing sickness cases. Lieutenant-Colonel Gowlland was ill with flu[439] so the acting C.O. of the 51st Field Ambulance was asked by the Colonel Barrow to submit requirements for the establishment of a Divisional Rest Station with beds for 150 patients at Château Bichecourt.[440] In general, in December, the Field Ambulance war diaries recorded the coming and going of medical personnel and it was the main business of most days.[441] Recording of incidents and events was certainly given the light touch. For

---

436 TNA: PRO. WO 95/1997. War Diary, 29th Mobile Veterinary Section, December - January 1916.

437 TNA: PRO. WO 95/1997. War Diary, 34th Sanitary Section, December 1916.

438 Personal Diary of Lieutenant-Colonel Fife.

439 He went sick with flu on 2 December and tried to return to work on 5 December. His devotion to his duty was admirable but as a senior doctor he should have known better. He was admitted to the New Zealand Stationary hospital at Amiens on 8 December where he remained until he had properly recovered. TNA: PRO. WO 95/1989. War Diary, A.D.M.S., December 1916.

440 TNA: PRO. WO 95/1989. War Diary, A.D.M.S., December 1916.

441 TNA: PRO. WO 95/1996. War Diary, 51st Field Ambulance, December 1916. & TNA: PRO. WO 95/1996, 52nd Field Ambulance, December 1916.

instance, the 52nd Field Ambulance briefly noted that on 8 December Captain A.V.J. Harrison, R.A.M.C., left the unit to return to Britain on the termination of his medical contract.[442] They failed to note that his refusal to renew his contract, which was unusual, had drawn the attention of the A.D.M.S., and the D.M.S., at Fourth Army. Harrison had even been interviewed twice at Fourth Army H.Q., but had still refused to renew his contract as a doctor in a Field Ambulance.[443] Their diary keeper also omitted to note that they were ordered by Colonel Barrow to send a medical officer to Cavillon on 9 December to attend another execution.[444] Rifleman Harry Poole of the 7th Yorks, who deserted on 3 October 1916, had been captured, court martialled, found guilty and sentenced to death. He was shot at dawn at Cavillon on 9 December 1916.[445]

Even when they returned to the line the Field Ambulances noted that all was quiet. For Lieutenant-Colonel Kay's 53rd Field Ambulance their story remained the same as they continued to care for, treat and evacuate the large numbers of sick at the XIV Corps Rest Station at Dive Copse.[446] If they hoped for relief at Dive Copse it was not going come soon. Orders came through from Corps, via Colonel Barrow telling them that they would remain at the Corps Rest Station for the foreseeable future.[447]

It would seem that the 17th Signal Company enjoyed their time out of the line. Indeed, they hardly bothered to keep a diary for

---

[442] TNA: PRO. WO 95/1996, 52nd Field Ambulance, December 1916.

[443] TNA: PRO. WO 95/1989. War Diary, A.D.M.S., November & December 1916. Harrison remained in the army as a doctor however. Perhaps he refused further overseas service.

[444] TNA: PRO. WO 95/1989. War Diary, A.D.M.S., December 1916.

[445] Poole had been Kitchener Volunteer and had been a member of the original battalion. He went out to the Western Front with the unit on 13 July 1915. He had been a miner before he joined up. His Medal Index Card records that he was a "Deserter." No mention of his desertion, his capture or of his execution, which would have been carried out by his own platoon, was mentioned in the battalion diary or in Lieutenant-Colonel Fife's diary. All of those British soldiers who were 'shot at dawn' in the Great War were granted Royal Pardons in 2006.

[446] TNA: PRO. WO 95/1996. War Diary, 53rd Field Ambulance, December 1916.

[447] TNA: PRO. WO 95/1989. War Diary, A.D.M.S., December 1916.

that period of time other than on 1 Dec, "Rest area and training." That entry was then followed by a column of dittos that look suspiciously like they were done all at the same time. This certainly was not the prescribed method of keeping war diaries![448] When they returned to the front line they noted that it was quiet and the communications were found to be good and held up remarkably well.[449] That would be because the guns were quiet.

Quality of the New Drafts

All units in the 17th Division needed reinforcement by this time. In fact all of the fighting divisions did. For example by the end of November 1916 the effective strength of the 7th Yorks was twenty-six officers and 754 NCOs and men.[450] The battalion was understrength by 350 men by the 1914/15 standard.[451] New drafts arrived and some were better quality than others and although, as we have seen, the likes of Lieutenant-Colonel Fife complained about some of the new drafts, the battalions had to take what they could get.[452] At least some of the new drafts that arrived in November and December 1916 had been soldiers for

---

[448] Staff Officers periodically raged about poor diary keeping. "Nothing to report" was a common entry that caused administrative complaints. However, when the divisional diary keeper typed the same words in the divisional diary such complaints by the staff often fell on deaf ears.

[449] TNA: PRO. WO 95/1994. War Diary, 17th Signal Company, December 1916.

[450] TNA: PRO. WO 95/2004. War Diary, 7th Yorks, November 1916.

[451] A battalion in 1914 and early 1915 would be between 1,000 and 1,100 officers and men strong.

[452] There was (and still is) a tendency to look back on the men who first volunteered for Kitchener's armies as statuesque, strong, clear eyed, healthy young men who soon became natural soldiers. By and large that was not true. A large number of Kitchener volunteers had been unfit, unhealthy and had struggled to become soldiers. The process to turn those civilians into soldiers had been long and arduous and some 1914 volunteers had only really learned to be soldiers by the time that they went into action for the first time on the Somme in July 1916. The well of volunteers had inevitably run dry by December 1915 so in December 1916 the battalions 'got what they were given.'

a time. Like the 137 men that turned up under the command of returning Captain Raymond Vivian Leslie Dallas[453] to join the 9th Northumberland Fusiliers on 11 December; they were largely Army Service Corps men.[454] The casualties caused by the Somme Campaign had forced the army to send rear echelon troops to the fighting battalions; often unfit and sometimes poorly trained in the arts of an infantryman. It also raises a small question about the wisdom of leaving, fit, healthy and well trained senior N.C.Os out of the line just because they were drill and gym instructors. The army answer would be that these N.C.Os would be able to turn the unfit soldiers into fit soldiers. Incidentally, Captain Stone, the 'old' officer that Fife complained about remained with the 7th Yorks and survived the war. It seems that the 'Bantams' remained as well and by the end of December the 7th Yorks had an effective strength of twenty-seven officers and 948 other ranks. The quality of the drafts might have been in question but these figures, if replicated across the division and the Corps, demonstrate that the manpower crisis was not, at that point in time, serious.[455]

As far as the 17th Division was concerned, quite apart from the officers and other ranks who had gone as "wastage"; killed, wounded, seconded or dismissed, the Somme had 'done for' one major-general,[456] three brigadier-generals[457] and a number of colonels. Therefore, when the units returned to the Somme

---

[453] Dallas was one of the battalion's original officers and had gone to France with it on 15 July 1915 as a lieutenant. He later earned the M.C., but was killed in action on 13 April 1918.

[454] TNA: PRO. WO 95/2013. War Diary, 9th Northumberland Fusiliers, December 1916.

[455] Of course, as the war progressed it would become a vexed issue for the B.E.F on the Western Front as the Navy and R.F.C., other theatres of war and industry demanded more man (and woman) power and the offensives caused higher and higher casualties.

[456] Major General T. D. Pilcher was dismissed on 12 July 1916. See Osborne, *Quadrangles, The 17th (Northern) Division On The Somme, 6 – 11 July 1916,* (Salient Books, 2010).

[457] Major-General Pilcher had dismissed Brigadier-General R. B. Fell in July 1916 just before being dismissed himself. See Osborne, *Quadrangles, The 17th (Northern) Division On The Somme, 6 – 11 July 1916,* (Salient Books, 2010).

front between 14 and 19 December eight out of the twelve battalions were commanded by majors.[458] In Brigadier-General Yatman's 50th Brigade the 7th Yorks were commanded by Lieutenant-Colonel Fife, the 7th East Yorks by Major King, the 10th West Yorks by Major Simner and the 6th Dorsets by Major Mairis.[459] In Brigadier-General Trotter's 51st brigade, the 7th Lincolns were commanded by Lieutenant-Colonel Metcalfe, the 10th Notts & Derbys by Major Gilbert, the 8th South Staffords by Major Tweedie and the 7th Borders by Major Irwin. In Brigadier-General Goodman's 52nd Brigade the 9th Northumberland Fusiliers were commanded by Lieutenant-Colonel Westmacott, the 12th Manchesters by Lieutenant-Colonel Magnay, the 9th Duke of Wellingtons, West Riding Regiment by Major Danby and the 10th Lancashire Fusiliers by Major Torrens.

In the Line/Return to the Line

When they returned to the line opposite Le Transloy in mid-December the Somme Campaign had been officially 'closed down' and the officers and men found that things had actually improved. [460] It was still cold and wet and there was still mud, but the artillery fire was less. Thanks to the Royal Engineers, who had not travelled to the rest area, the camps were now furnished with Nissen Huts[461] and trackways were duckboard paths raised above the mud and water on piles making the trip to and from the front much easier and safer. Water could still fill the trenches but improved pumps could handle most floods.[462]

---

[458] Although a number of these men were soon promoted to Lieutenant-Colonel.

[459] He commanded the battalion until replaced by a regular officer of the Dorset Regiment and former staff officer at General Headquarters, Major A. L. Moulton-Barrett, in January 1917.

[460] IWM: Mozley, 01/48/1.

[461] TNA: PRO. WO 95/1993. War Diary, 78th Field Company, R.E. November & December 1916.

[462] O' Hanlon, A Plain History of the Sixth (Service) Battalion, p. 126.

Water pipes had been laid to forward areas and bath houses making it easier to get clean and to obtain fresh water.[463] The front line was safer, machine gun fire and sniping from the German lines was infrequent and consequently the British were quieter as well. There were no offensive operations, the line was held and improved.

For this tour the division was divided into two Brigade groups each of six battalions, thereby giving one brigade staff a clear rest in rotation.[464] Only 400 men per battalion went into the line, and they spread out along a frontage of one mile. In the line men hardly moved during their 48-hour stint; they got into position and remained where they were.[465] Those not in the line were employed in construction, sapping and road mending.[466] The light railways, under construction to improve the flow of men and munitions to and from the line, also provided plenty of work for the troops who were out of the line.[467]

Trench Foot and illness still sent men to hospital but foot rubbing parades were regularly carried out, more gumboots were issued and the duck walk paths began to improve foot conditions. 'Foot Friction Drill' was often recorded, possibly to show that something was being done to combat the condition and that orders were being followed,[468] but no figures appear for Trench Foot casualties in the battalion diaries for this time. Nor do the Field Ambulances record men admitted for the condition. The XIV Corps Rest Station at Dive Copse sometimes had somewhere in the region of 1,000 patients from across the Corps; perhaps some of these were Trench Foot cases but if they were they were not recorded as such. Although, to be fair to the 53rd Field Ambulance they did not record the kinds of sickness

463 TNA: PRO. WO 95/1993. War Diary, 93rd Field Company, R.E. November & December 1916.
464 Hoyte, *10th (S) Battalion*, p. 24.
465 Hoyte, *10th (S) Battalion*, p. 24.
466 Hoyte, *10th (S) Battalion*, p. 24.
467 IWM: Mozley, 01/48/1.
468 TNA: PRO. WO 95/2002. War Diary, 7th East Yorks, December 1916.

that their patients suffered from. It really does seem that Trench Foot was a taboo subject and no one wanted to talk about it in official paperwork.

In December the 7th Lincolns introduced some interesting measures to combat Trench Foot and make sure that the men rubbed oil into their feet, "Certificates that feet have been rubbed and oiled will be required at 12 noon tomorrow. Each man will dip his socks into a pan of hot fat, put them on when they are cool, to march out of camp in."[469] How long certificating feet and dipping socks lasted is anyone's guess.[470]

Of course Trench Foot was not eradicated and even Lieutenant-Colonel Fife found himself defending his battalion against 50th Brigade H.Q. when the number of cases rose in the 7th Yorks during December. However, Fife, the senior Colonel in 50th Brigade and nominal brigade 2 i/c, who was popular with Major-General Robertson and tipped for promotion to Brigadier-General, remained in post.[471] This also proved that even a very good battalion like the 7th Yorks could suffer from Trench Foot and that an excellent C.O., like Fife could do little to stop the condition if it took hold. It does look as if Rowley and Soames had been unfairly treated.

Decent footwear went a good way to fending off Trench Foot; the Tommies knew it and the more capable and enterprising often took it upon themselves to beat the dreaded condition. One afternoon in the trenches, Captain Mozley reprimanded

---

[469] TNA: PRO. WO 95/2007. War Diary, 7th Lincolns, December 1916.

[470] On the matter of certificates and considering that the divisional staff were on the 'warpath' about the state of billets and the furniture the 7th Lincolns instituted and operated a certificate system for the billets to prove that they were whole and in good order.

[471] Fife was wounded by a 5.9-inch shell on 13 February 1917. His left arm was broken in three places and he was deafened. His wounds took years to heal, he never returned to his unit or to the fighting and he remained deaf for the rest of his life. He did, however, join the Home Guard in WW II as a private soldier. His C.O. was his own gamekeeper. From the Personal diary of Lieutenant-Colonel Fife.

Sergeant George V. Crumpler[472] for wearing a pair of immaculate lace up German field boots, "which he had pinched from a dead German officer."[473] Sergeant Crumpler, the senior N.C.O in Mozley's A Company, listened as his officer scolded him and then pointed out to Mozley "that it was a pity that they should be wasted."[474] Mozley agreed with Crumpler's point, after all he hardly held the moral high ground. Mozley admitted that as he admonished Crumpler he himself was wearing a superb pair of privately purchased Lotus Veldtschoen (to replace a pair burned by a flare) and they were keeping his feet comfortably warm and dry.[475] Crumpler was not in a position to buy his own boots and so had to resort to other methods to improve his lot. If Sergeant Crumpler heeded Captain Mozley's words is not recorded.

Throughout the Somme Campaign the British seemed to a have been fighting up hill, under observation and often in salient, but by December there was a sense that the British were gaining the upper hand. On Boxing Day,

> *A decent strafe by our guns was started at midday, directed chiefly against the German trenches in front of Le Transloy. These positions were almost in dead ground, as far as observation from our trench was concerned, but we could see from our maps, that a strongly wired trench ran in front of the village. Le Transloy could, of course, be seen, and for once we were top dog and could bring direct fire to bear on the German communications.[476]*

Indeed, the German troops opposite seemed to have lost the vigour and professionalism that they had displayed in earlier

---

[472] Sergeant Crumpler had gone out to the Western Front on 13 July 1915 as a corporal and was one of the battalion's original Kitchener Volunteers. He was promoted to Company Sergeant Major and on 28 December 1918 he was Mentioned in Despatches.

[473] IWM: Mozley, 01/48/1.

[474] IWM: Mozley, 01/48/1.

[475] These boots are still on sale today. The name is Afrikaans and dates from the Boer War, the boots were very popular with officers during the Great War.

[476] IWM: Mozley, 01/48/1.

months. In the early hours of Boxing Day B Company of the 7th East Yorks saw a party of about 50 German soldiers "in full marching order advancing towards our front line." They were allowed to get almost on top of the British trench when Captain Henry Sherard Osborn Ashington,[477] "who talks German"[478] called out to them and ordered them to put up their hands and surrender. Eighteen of them complied and came into the British trench, the rest turned and made for their own lines. Whereupon the "left company turned on a Lewis Gun, and all available rifles and must have killed most of them."[479] The eighteen prisoners and a few of the wounded who could be rounded up from no-man's-land came from the 121st Reserve Infantry Regiment and were part of a trench relief that had lost their way in the darkness and advanced straight into the British line.

Although the prisoners would give up some valuable intelligence it was not a particularly remarkable happening and the 17th Division war diary keeper noted that on 26 December there was "no event of importance to record."[480] What was remarkable was that Lieutenant-Colonel King felt the need to point out to 50th Brigade H.Q. that *his* men had captured the Germans soldiers; *not* the 12th Manchesters who escorted them to the cage. He said, "The eighteen prisoners were sent back at once under a guard of 4 other ranks but they got into the 12th Manchesters rear or support trenches, and this regiment took them over and undertook to deliver them to Divisional Post."[481] Not that the 12th Manchester actually claimed them, they just inferred that the

---

477 Ashington was one of the battalion's original officers and had come to the Western Front on 14 July 1915. He was killed in action, age 25, on 31 January 1917.

478 Lieutenant-Colonel East King in TNA: PRO. WO 95/2002. War Diary, 7th East Yorks, December 1916.

479 Lieutenant-Colonel East King in TNA: PRO. WO 95/2002. War Diary, 7th East Yorks, December 1916.

480 TNA: PRO. WO 95/1981. War Diary, 17th Division, December 1916.

481 Lieutenant-Colonel East King in TNA: PRO. WO 95/2002. War Diary, 7th East Yorks, December 1916.

East Yorks had not provided an adequate escort. Their diary keeper wrote, "18 prisoners were brought in during the early morning by an officer of East Yorks and we provided an escort to conduct them to the rear area."[482] The small episode drew congratulations from Major-General Robertson himself who wrote that he, "wishes to congratulate all ranks of the 7th Btn E. Yorks who were concerned in the capture of the party of Germans on the night of 25th/26th December. He considers that Captain Ashington handled the situation very well."[483] It was Major-General Robertson's way of smoothing ruffled feathers and saying that he knew very well which battalion had taken the prisoners.

The men of the division held the line on what was rapidly becoming the peaceful Somme front but the soldiers in all of the battalions and units were beginning to show signs of exhaustion as the end of the year approached.[484] Men were continuing to fall ill. In November and December, probably paying the price for constant repair and construction work, Captain Robert Charles Lundie's[485] 93rd Field Company, R.E., recorded a steady stream of men, in ones and twos, going sick and being admitted to hospital.[486] Captain Mozley's infantry company was no exception; Mozley himself remembered throwing up in the back of a trench but he put it down to drinking strange smelling water from a petrol can. One of his officers, Second Lieutenant H. Butler suffering from lumbago, was granted leave beginning on New Year's Eve. Mozley was sorry to see him go but he acknowledged that Butler had been ill for some time and could

---

[482] TNA: PRO. WO 95/2012. War Diary, 12th Manchesters, December 1916.

[483] TNA: PRO. WO 95/2002. War Diary, 7th East Yorks, December 1916.

[484] Personal Diary of Lieutenant-Colonel Fife.

[485] Lundie had been a Royal Engineer lieutenant in the Special Reserve and went out to the Western Front with the 17th Division on 15 July 1915. He was promoted to Captain and then Major, Mentioned in Despatches 15 June 1916 and 23 July 1917 and awarded the D.S.O. He was killed in action on either 14 or 15 October 1918.

[486] TNA: PRO. WO 95/1993. War Diary, 93rd Field Company R.E., November & December 1916.

not spend another day in the trenches.[487] By now Captain Mozley was the only officer left in A Company, which was now 150 men strong,[488] and the platoons were commanded by N.C.Os. His fellow officers had disappeared one by one. Lieutenant J. A. W. MacMullen[489] had gone to the divisional works battalion which had been created in late November by taking 60 men from each of the division's fighting battalions.[490] Lieutenant C.C.C. Case had gone sick,[491] Second Lieutenant R. K. Holt was on a course,[492] Second Lieutenant A.C.W Hands had also gone on leave,[493] and Second Lieutenant Harold Chermside[494] had been seconded to the R.F.A.[495] Therefore, when Butler bade them farewell, Sergeant Crumpler became Captain Mozley's 2 i/c.

On 31 December it was very quiet on the Somme. No machine gun fire, no rifle fire, just a very few shells.[496] Of New Year's Eve Captain Mozley wrote,

At 11 p.m., which corresponded to the German midnight, a rare old strafe was started by our guns ... All round, in a wide sweep, the

---

487   IWM: Mozley, 01/48/1.

488   IWM: Mozley, 01/48/1.

489   Another Kitchener Volunteer veteran. Lieutenant MacMullen had been a C.S.M in January 1916 when he was Mentioned in Despatches. He rose to the rank of captain and survived the war.

490   TNA: PRO. WO 95/2005. War Diary, 51st Brigade, November 1916.

491   Case had gone out to the Western Front as a Second Lieutenant in the 1st Gloucesters. His Medal Index Card then records that he was a Lieutenant in the 3rd Dorsets and makes no mention of his service in the 6th Battalion. Case survived the war and remained in the army.

492   Holt rose to the rank of lieutenant and survived the war. He was awarded the Silver War Badge on 19 September 1919.

493   Hands rose to the rank of captain and survived the war.

494   He remained with the Royal Field Artillery. Chermside had gone out to the Western Front as a private in the 7th Dragoon Guards on 13 October 1914. He transferred to the infantry and joined the 3rd Dorsets as a sergeant on 3 June 1915 and was commissioned into that regiment on 6 February 1916. He rose to the rank of lieutenant and survived the war.

495   This was, including Captain Mozley, a lucky band of company officers; they all survived the war.

496   TNA: PRO. WO 95/2014. War Diary, 9th Duke of Wellingtons, West Riding Regiment, December 1916.

horizon was aflame, and the year 1917 was ushered in to the sound of our shells crashing on to the German positions. As far as I could see there was little retaliation.[497]

On the Somme, on the following day, 1 January 1917, life, death and work carried on as normal.[498] Captain Mozley was wounded on 2 January and his time on the Western Front was over.[499] Sergeant Crumpler became company commander.

The pick of the Brigades had been the 51st Brigade, it had put in the effort and succeeded and Brigadier-General Trotter kept his job.[500] There was a marked difference in the way that the brigades operated. At Zenith Trench orders to attack, if possible, were given by 51st Brigade and when the battalion's answer was affirmative permission to attack was granted by brigade without recourse to 17th Division or XIV Corps H.Qs. In contrast at Finch Trench permission for the 7th Yorks second attack was passed along the chain of command by 50th Brigade and it went right up to XIV Corps level before the orders were cancelled. The decision that could have been made at brigade level took too long and it was too late for the countermand order to stop the attack. The 52nd Brigade did nothing offensive at all.

It was all over for the 17th Division in the Somme Campaign of 1916. They had fought from Quadrangle Support Trench, between Contalmaison and Mametz Wood in July, on to the splintered remains of Delville Wood in August and finished up

---

497 IWM: Mozley, 01/48/1.

498 Personal Diary of Lieutenant-Colonel Fife.

499 He was wounded in the leg by shell splinter on New Year's Day, 1917 and although he made light of the wound in his memoir he was shipped back to hospital in Britain and never went out to the Western Front again. The splinter was removed on 19 January 1917. Once recovered he was posted, on 11 May 1917, to the 11th Officer Cadet Battalion at Pirbright where he remained for the rest of the war. He stayed in the Army after the war and was a permanent Captain in 1921.

500 Trotter was Mentioned in Despatches on 15 May 1917 and by the war's end had been awarded the C.B., C.M.G., M.V.O., and D.S.O. In 1918 he had a prestigious post in the United States of America at The British Military Mission, 703, Fifteenth Street, Washington D.C.

in a sea of freezing mud near Le Transloy in November. A distance, from Quadrangle Support to the front line opposite Le Transloy, as the crow flies, of a little over six miles. The 17th Division was due back in the line in December and by the time it returned the Somme Campaign had been officially 'closed down' on 18 November. By which time the weather and ground conditions had become even worse, the frost having given way to heavy rain.[501] Everyone expected the campaign to start again in the New Year, not that the sniping, shelling and patrolling actually ceased, but the German Army had other ideas. They were pulling back to their new line and were about to give the devastated wasteland and the sea of mud to the B.E.F., and the French Army. In 1917 the Battles of Arras and Passchendaele awaited the 17th (Northern) Division.

The 17th Division's star might well have been on the rise by the end of 1916. Their training had impressed General Allenby and Third Army while serving up at Gommecourt, Major-General Robertson had acted decisively to combat the Trench Foot epidemic that broke out in the 50th Brigade and the successful operations at Zenith Trench had brought the formation praise from General Rawlinson and the Fourth Army Staff. With the New Year would come new offensives and a prestigious role for the division at the opening of the Battle of Arras.

---

[501] TNA: PRO. WO 95/911. War Diary, XIV Corps, November, 1916.

Casualties

This appendix is not an exhaustive list of the 17th Division's casualties during the September tour at Gommecourt or the October/November/December 1916 tours of duty opposite Le Transloy. It deals with infantry battalion deaths that mainly occurred during the operations discussed in the text. There were many more men who died of wounds or died.

5 September 1916

4th Battalion, Special Brigade, R.E.

Aris, Sidney Victor, Pioneer, 129186. KIA by shellfire during a British gas attack aged 19. Born in and a resident of Richmond, Surrey. Son of George and Kate Aris. Buried in grave I. M. 6 in Foncquevillers Military Cemetery.

Griffith, John, Pioneer, 130579. KIA by shellfire during a British gas attack. Formerly, 4231 Griffith of the Royal Welch Fusiliers. Born in Llanenddwyn, Merionethshire, Wales. A resident of Dyffryn, Merionethshire and enlisted in Barmouth, Merionethshire. There appears to be no burial or commemoration information for this man.

29 October 1916

First tour in the trenches on the return to the Somme. The men of the 10th West Yorks recorded as killed on 29, 30, 31 October and 1, 2, November were all killed by shelling or sniping.

Gott, Fred, 28747, Lance Corporal. KIA probably by shellfire during the relief of the 2nd Yorks. In fact his Medal Index Card records that he was presumed dead on this date. Born in Saltaire, Yorkshire and enlisted in Bingley Yorkshire. Arrived on the Western Front after 31 December 1915. Commemorated on Thiepval Memorial, Pier and Face, 2A, 2C and 2D.

Handley, Robert, Private, 13816. KIA by shellfire during the relief of the 2nd West Yorks. Age 46. Born in Barrowby, Lincolnshire. Enlisted in and a resident of Sheffield. The son of Andrew and Mary Handley and the husband of Mrs. L. Handley, 81, Alfred Road, Brightside, Sheffield. A Kitchener Volunteer who came out to the Western Front on 10 September 1915 and, therefore, probably a survivor of 1 July 1916. Buried in Guards Cemetery, Lesboeufs in grave, VII. Q. 4.

30 October 1916

10thWest Yorks

Atkinson, Samuel Smilley, Lance Corporal, 3/9642. Killed in action. Born and enlisted in Leeds. Arrived on the Western Front after 31 December 1915. Commemorated on Thiepval Memorial, Pier and Face, 2A, 2C and 2D.

Atkinson, William, Private, 43267. Killed in action. Age 20. Born in Hetton-Le-Hole and enlisted in Houghton-Le-Spring, Durham. Arrived on the Western Front after 31 December 1915. The son of John and Elizabeth Atkinson of 108A, Houghton Road, Hetton-Le-Hole. Commemorated on Thiepval Memorial, Pier and Face, 2A, 2C and 2D.

Briggs, William Arthur, Private, 43701. Killed in action. A resident of Dunnington York and enlisted in York. Arrived on the Western Front after 31 December 1915. Commemorated on Thiepval Memorial, Pier and Face, 2A, 2C and 2D.

Kingston, Joseph, Private, 21815. Killed in action. Age 35. Born and enlisted in West Hartlepool. Arrived on the Western Front after 31 December 1915. Son of Susannah and John Kingston, 45, Albert Street, West Hartlepool. Commemorated on Thiepval Memorial, Pier and Face, 2A, 2C and 2D.

Levi, Barnet, Private, 25660. Killed in action. Age 33. Born and enlisted in Leeds. Son of Betsy and Max Levi of 13, St. Peter's Square, Leeds. Arrived on the Western Front after 31 December 1915. Commemorated on Thiepval Memorial, Pier and Face, 2A, 2C and 2D.

Mawhinney, George, Private, 43251. Killed in action. Age 21. Born in Haswell, Durham and enlisted in Chester-Le-Street, Durham. Formerly, Private, 31784, 4th Durham Light Infantry. Arrived on the Western Front after 31 December 1915. Son of Mr and Mrs John Mawhinney of 8, Boston Street, Easington Colliery, County Durham. Commemorated on Thiepval Memorial, Pier and Face, 2A, 2C and 2D.

Metcalfe, Henry Norris, Private, 43285. Killed in action. Age 30. Born and enlisted in Gateshead. Arrived on the Western Front after 31 December 1915. Son of William Middleton and Clara Jane Metcalfe of 32, Kingsborough Terrace, Gateshead-On-Tyne. Commemorated on Thiepval Memorial, Pier and Face, 2A, 2C and 2D.

Nicholls, Robert Edgar, Private, 43170. Killed in action. Age 21. Born in Leeds and enlisted in Hull. Formerly, 1181, 3rd East Yorks. Arrived on the Western Front after 31 December 1915. Son of Robert and Emily Nicholls. Buried in Delville Wood Cemetery, Longueval in grave, VII. O. 7.

Stansfield, Thomas, Private, 43202. A Company. Killed in action. Age 25. Born and enlisted in Leeds. Recorded on his Medal Index Card as presumed dead. Arrived on the Western Front after 31 December 1915. Son of Annie E. Stansfield of 10, Charlton Grove, East Park Road, Leeds. Commemorated on Thiepval Memorial, Pier and Face, 2A, 2C and 2D.

Taylor, George Edward, Private 43138. D Company. Killed in action. Age 23. Born and enlisted in Hull. Formerly, Private, 941, 5th East Yorks Cycle Corps. Arrived on the Western Front after 31 December 1915. Son of John Thomas and Ellen Mary Taylor of "Hawthorne", Anlaby Park, Hull. Commemorated on Thiepval Memorial, Pier and Face, 2A, 2C and 2D.

Wood, Alfred William, Private, 43265. Died of wounds. Born in Alnwick, Northumberland and enlisted in Gateshead. Formerly, Private, 31554, Durham Light Infantry. The list of soldiers' effects records that Wood died sometime between 30 October and 1 November 1916, despite being in the D.L.I. he did not come out to the Western Front until after 31 December 1915. Commemorated on Thiepval Memorial, Pier and Face, 2A, 2C and 2D

31 October 1916

10th West Yorks.

Ashton, William, Private, 43307. Died of Wounds after being wounded by shellfire on either 29 or 30 October. Born in Belper, Derbyshire. A resident of Holmwood, Derbyshire and enlisted in Chesterfield. Formerly, Private, 18489, Yorks and Lancs and arrived at Gallipoli on 12 October 1915. Commemorated on Thiepval Memorial, Pier and Face, 2A, 2C and 2D.

Taylor, George Henry, Private, 43299. Died of wounds. Born and enlisted in Hull. Formerly, Private, 13/1117, East Yorks and he arrived in Egypt on 29 December 1915. Commemorated on Thiepval Memorial, Pier and Face, 2A, 2C and 2D.

Warringham, Andrew, Private, 43332. Killed in action. Age 35. Born in Penistone, Barnsley, Yorkshire. A resident of, and enlisted in Sheffield. Formerly, Private, 4631, Yorks and Lancs and arrived at Gallipoli on 11 July 1915. Husband of Lily Beeley (formerly Warringham) of 29, Green Lane, Sheffield. Commemorated on Thiepval Memorial, Pier and Face, 2A, 2C and 2D.

Willford, Arthur Chester, Private, 43160. Killed in action. Age 35. Enlisted in Hull. Formerly, Private 5421, East Yorks. Arrived on the Western Front after 31 December 1915. Son of James Richardson Willford. Buried in Guards Cemetery, Lesboeufs in grave, III. ZZ. 10.

1 November 1916

10th West Yorks

Charlesworth, Joseph Henry, Private, 43186. Died of wounds. Born in Nottingly, Yorkshire and enlisted in Leeds. Arrived on the Western Front after 31 December 1915. Commemorated on Thiepval Memorial, Pier and Face, 2A, 2C and 2D.

Hunter, Edward, Private, 40129. Killed in action. Age 20. Born and enlisted in Sunderland. Son of Mr. T and Mrs. E Hunter of 12, Ayre's Quay Street, Deptford, Sunderland. Arrived on the Western Front after 31 December 1915. Buried in Guards Cemetery Lesboeufs in grave, XI. V. 10.

Ridley, Tom, Private 28601. Killed in action. Age 19. Born and enlisted in Bradford. Son of Thomas Ridley of 12, Lake Street, Oxford. Arrived on the Western Front after 31 December 1915.

Commemorated on Thiepval Memorial, Pier and Face, 2A, 2C and 2D.

Sullivan, Francis, Private, 23284. Killed in action. Born and enlisted in York. Arrived on the Western Front after 31 December 1915. Commemorated on Thiepval Memorial, Pier and Face, 2A, 2C and 2D.

Toulson, William, Private, 12762. Died of wounds. Born and enlisted in Leeds. Husband of E. Toulson of 23 Nellie View, Richmond Hill, Leeds. One of the original Kitchener Volunteers of this battalion who came out to the Western Front with the 17th Division on 13 July 1915 and, therefore, probably a survivor of 1 July 1916. Buried in London Road Cemetery and Extension, Longueval in grave, 9. D. 41.

Watts, Enoch, Private, 17374. Killed in action. Born in Chesterfield and enlisted in Sheffield. Formerly Private 15182, East Yorks. A Kitchener Volunteer who came out to the Western Front on 10 September 1915 and, therefore, probably a survivor of 1 July 1916. Commemorated on Thiepval Memorial, Pier and Face, 2A, 2C and 2D.

2 November 1916

10th West Yorks

Atkinson, Herbert, Private, 21876. Died of wounds. Born and enlisted in Huddersfield. Arrived on the Western Front after 31 December 1915. Buried in Grove Town Cemetery, Meaulte in grave II. F. 40.

Blackwell, Alfred, Private, 28745. Killed in action. Born in Kirby Moorside, Yorkshire and enlisted in Yeadon. Arrived on the Western Front after 31 December 1915. Commemorated on Thiepval Memorial, Pier and Face, 2A, 2C and 2D.

Cooper, Percy, Private 16051. A Company. Killed in action. Age 23. Born in Kendal, Worcester and enlisted in Birmingham. Son of Walter and Elizabeth Cooper of "Thornhaugh", New Road, Rubery, Birmingham. One of the original Kitchener Volunteers of this battalion who came out to the Western Front with the 17th Division on 13 July 1915 and, therefore, probably a survivor of 1 July 1916. Commemorated on Thiepval Memorial, Pier and Face, 2A, 2C and 2D.

Mennell, Roy Walter, Private 43101. Killed in action. Born in York and enlisted in Hull. Arrived on the Western Front after 31 December 1915. Commemorated on Thiepval Memorial, Pier and Face, 2A, 2C and 2D.

Woodward, William Robinson, Private, 24683. Age 24. Killed in action. Born in Knaresborough, Yorkshire and enlisted in Harrogate. Son of Sarah Ann and Benjamin Woodward of Coronation House, Kirkgate, Knaresborough, Arrived on the Western Front after 31 December 1915. Commemorated on Thiepval Memorial, Pier and Face, 2A, 2C and 2D.

Zenith Trench Operation Casualties

2 November 1916

7th Borders

Jackson, Arthur, Second Lieutenant. KIA. From Whitehaven, Cumberland. Buried in Bancourt British Cemetery, in grave III. H. 12.

3 November 1916

7th Borders

Hart, Frederick Arthur, 8760, Lance Corporal. KIA. Born in Reading, Berkshire and enlisted in Canterbury, Kent. Buried in A.I.F. Burial Ground, Flers in grave I. D. 22.

7th Lincolns

Atkin, Ernest, 21471, Private. KIA. Born and enlisted in Grimsby, Lincolnshire. Age 25. The son of Mr and Mrs. Atkin, 71, Annesley Street, West Marsh, Grimsby. Commemorated on Thiepval Memorial, Pier and Face, 1 C.

Cooper, John Charles, 14904, Sergeant, M.M. KIA. Born and enlisted in Gainsborough, Lincolnshire. Commemorated on Thiepval Memorial, Pier and Face, 1 C.

Davy, Fred, 19152, Private. KIA. Born in and a resident of Wainfleet, Lincolnshire and enlisted in Lincoln. Commemorated on Thiepval Memorial, Pier and Face, 1 C.

Foster, Anson, 12788, Private. KIA. Born in Hanley, Staffordshire and enlisted in Stoke on Trent. Commemorated on Thiepval Memorial, Pier and Face, 1 C.

Hayes, Charles Henry, 18788, Lance Corporal. KIA. Born in Boston, Lincolnshire and a resident of Ragnall, Nottinghamshire. Enlisted in Newark. Commemorated on Thiepval Memorial, Pier and Face, 1 C.

King, Harold, 12986, Private. KIA. Born in Louth, Lincolnshire and a resident of Howerby, Lincolnshire. Enlisted in Louth. Commemorated on Thiepval Memorial, Pier and Face, 1 C.

Moore, Arthur, 19288, Lance Corporal. KIA. Born in Market Deeping, Lincolnshire and resident of Deeping St. James, Lincolnshire. Enlisted in Bourne, Lincolnshire. Age 33. Commemorated on Thiepval Memorial, Pier and Face, 1 C.

Page, Sydney, 23419, Private. KIA. Born in Grimsby and a resident of Cleethorpes, Lincolnshire. Enlisted in Grimsby. Age 26. Commemorated on Thiepval Memorial, Pier and Face, 1 C.

Parker, Philip, 22628, Private. KIA. Born in Stickford, Lincolnshire and a resident of Wrangle Lincolnshire. Enlisted in Boston. Commemorated on Thiepval Memorial, Pier and Face, 1 C.

Pask, Harry, 12032, Private. KIA. Born in Slipton, Northants and enlisted in Spalding, Lincolnshire. Commemorated on Thiepval Memorial, Pier and Face, 1 C.

Potter, Charles, 8535, Sergeant. KIA. Born in Brothertoft, Lincolnshire and a resident of Boston. Enlisted in Lincoln. Age 26. Commemorated on Thiepval Memorial, Pier and Face, 1 C.

Rhodes, George, 12952, Corporal. KIA. Born in and a resident of Peterborough, Northants. Enlisted in Boston. Commemorated on Thiepval Memorial, Pier and Face, 1 C.

Robinson, John Edward, Second Lieutenant. KIA. Formerly DM/07542 Lance Corporal Robinson in the ASC. He arrived on the Western Front on 28 August 1916 presumably when he joined the 7th Lincolns. Age 31. Buried in grave, IV. O. 10 Guards' Cemetery Les Boeufs.

Rose, Arthur, 22767, Private. KIA. Born in Epworth Lincolnshire and enlisted in Althorpe, Lincolnshire. Commemorated on Thiepval Memorial, Pier and Face, 1 C.

Rossington, John, 18046, Private. KIA. Born and enlisted in Lincoln. Commemorated on Thiepval Memorial, Pier and Face, 1 C.

Sharpe, John Herbert, 22872, Private. KIA. Born in and a resident of Newborough, Northants. Enlisted in Lincoln. Commemorated on Thiepval Memorial, Pier and Face, 1 C.

Snart, George, 22588, Private. KIA. Born in and a resident of Baston, Lincolnshire. Enlisted in Bourne, Lincolnshire. Age 23. Commemorated on Thiepval Memorial, Pier and Face, 1 C.

Sparling, Walter William, 22572, Private. KIA. Born in Grimsby and enlisted in Lincoln. Commemorated on Thiepval Memorial, Pier and Face, 1 C.

Spinks, Thomas, 22675, Private. KIA. Born Holbeach, Lincolnshire and a resident of Long Sutton, Lincolnshire. Enlisted in Lincoln. Age 19. Commemorated on Thiepval Memorial, Pier and Face, 1 C.

Starsmore, Thomas Bean, 22854, Private. KIA. Born in and a resident of Baston, Lincolnshire. Enlisted in Bourne. Commemorated on Thiepval Memorial, Pier and Face, 1 C.

Sweet, Samuel, 18167, Private. KIA. Born in Plymouth, Devon and a resident of Devonport. Enlisted in Sutton-in-Ashfield. Age 30, Commemorated on Thiepval Memorial, Pier and Face, 1 C.

Tindall, James, 13431, Lance Corporal. KIA. Born in and a resident of Dunstan, Lincolnshire. Enlisted in Lincoln. Age 21. Commemorated on Thiepval Memorial, Pier and Face, 1 C.

Wilson, Arthur, 10675, Private. KIA. Born and enlisted in Nottingham. Buried in London Cemetery and extension, Longeuval in grave 1. C. 1.

52nd Brigade attack on the German Strong Point and counter-attack.

10th Lancashire Fusiliers

Almon, Jesse, 5690, Private. KIA. A resident of Kenfig Hill, Glamorgan and enlisted in Bridgend. Commemorated on Thiepval Memorial, Pier and Face, 3 C and 3D.

Goulding, Herbert, 5055, R.S.M., M.C., KIA. Born and enlisted in Bury and a resident of Barrow-in-Furness. His death date is given as 4 November 1916 but the battalion war diary records it as 3 November. Commemorated on Thiepval Memorial, Pier and Face, 3 C and 3D.

Hoskins, George, Second Lieutenant. KIA. 3rd Battalion attached to 10th Battalion. Age 21. Son of John Thomas and Anne Hoskins of 'Thornleigh', Penwortham, Preston. His death date is given as 5 November 1916 but the battalion war diary records it as 3 November. Buried in Longueval Road Cemetery in grave I. 18.

McHugh, Charles, 5309, Sergeant. KIA. Born in Heywood, Lancashire and a resident of Chadderton. Enlisted in Oldham. Commemorated on Thiepval Memorial, Pier and Face, 3 C and 3D.

Timms, Edward, 39885, Private. KIA. Born in Stockport and enlisted in Aston-Under-Lyne. Age 25. The son of Joseph and Annie Timms, 5 Barlow Row, Hillgate, Stockport. Commemorated on Thiepval Memorial, Pier and Face, 3 C and 3D.

Townend, Norman, 34841, Private. KIA. Born in Windhill, Yorkshire and enlisted in Blackburn. Age 23. The son of R. W. and Ellen Townend of 20 Granville Road, Blackburn.

Commemorated on Thiepval Memorial, Pier and Face, 3 C and 3D.

Watterson, John, 5421, Private. KIA. Born in Castletown, Douglas, the Isle of Man and enlisted in Douglas. Age 21. Son of John and Anna Watterson, Garden Cottage, Castletown, the Isle of Man. Commemorated on Thiepval Memorial, Pier and Face, 3 C and 3D.

York, Thomas, 3990, Private. KIA. Born in and a resident of Cardiff. Enlisted in Ashton-Under-Lyne. Commemorated on Thiepval Memorial, Pier and Face, 3 C and 3D.

4 November 1916

R.A.M.C., 51st Field Ambulance.

Brown, Joseph, 38039, Private, KIA by shellfire. Born and enlisted in Bolton, Lancashire. Commemorated on Thiepval Memorial, Pier and Face, 4 C.

Finch and Orion Trench Operations.

5 November 1916

7th Yorks. (Yorkshire Hussars, Alexandra, Princess of Wales Own).

Barrow, Joseph, 19099, Private. KIA. Born and enlisted in South Shields. Age 31. Commemorated on Thiepval Memorial, Pier and Face, 3 A and 3 D.

Bentley, Arthur, 3/8725. Private. KIA. Born in Melbourne, Yorkshire and enlisted in Middlesbrough. Age 34. Buried in London Cemetery and Extension, Longeuval in grave, 7. F. 21.

Campbell, William, 14880, Private. KIA. Born and enlisted in South Shields. Commemorated on Thiepval Memorial, Pier and Face, 3 A and 3 D.

Crisp, Errol, 26371, Private. KIA. Born in South Bank, Yorkshire and enlisted in Thirsk, Yorkshire. Commemorated on Thiepval Memorial, Pier and Face, 3 A and 3 D.

Dennis, John William, 23486, Private. KIA. Born in Stokesley, Yorkshire and enlisted in West Hartlepool. Age 21. Commemorated on Thiepval Memorial, Pier and Face, 3 A and 3 D.

Fearon, Michael, 3/7413, Private. KIA. Born and enlisted in Middlesbrough. Commemorated on Thiepval Memorial, Pier and Face, 3 A and 3 D.

Goldsmith, Lewis Wilberforce, Captain. KIA. Commemorated on Thiepval Memorial, Pier and Face, 3 A and 3 D.

Goodall, A. C., Second Lieutenant. KIA. The son of Robert and Emily Sarah Goodall. Age 22. The *Service Medal and Awards Roll* records that Second Lieutenant A. C. Goodall of the 7th Yorks was killed in action on the night of 5/6 November 1916. The *Army Registers of Soldiers' Effect* records that he was killed in action on 6 November 1916. His commanding officer's report and the war diary record that he was killed in action on 5 November 1916. Commemorated on Thiepval Memorial, Pier and Face, 3 A and 3 D.

Harrison, William, 3/7103, Corporal. KIA. Born in Lazenby, Eston, Yorkshire and enlisted in Middlesbrough. Age 27. Buried in Guards Cemetery, Lesboeufs in grave, VI. ZZ. 3.

Healey, James, 27223, Private. KIA. Born in Middlesbrough and enlisted in Stockton on Tees. Commemorated on Thiepval Memorial, Pier and Face, 3 A and 3 D.

Hemingway, John Arnold, 18451, Private. KIA. Born and enlisted in Dewsbury, Yorkshire. Formerly in the Yorkshire

Light Infantry. Age 26. Commemorated on Thiepval Memorial, Pier and Face, 3 A and 3 D.

Hill, Roland, 16610, Private. KIA. Born in Ferryhill and enlisted in Sunderland. Buried in Bancourt British Cemetery in grave III. D. 3.

Lee, Tom, 24395, Private. KIA. Born and enlisted in Stokesley. Commemorated on Thiepval Memorial, Pier and Face, 3 A and 3 D.

Moore, Simon, 20541, Private. KIA. Born in Hardean, Yorkshire and enlisted in Leyburn. Buried in Sucrerie Military Cemetery, Colincamps in grave II. A. 13.

Pattison, Thomas Edward, 17840, Sergeant. KIA. Born and enlisted in Seaham Harbour. Commemorated on Thiepval Memorial, Pier and Face, 3 A and 3 D.

Porter, James, 18235, Lance Corporal. KIA. Born in Eldon Colliery, Durham and a resident of Easington Colliery, Durham. Enlisted in Sunderland. Age 21. Commemorated on Thiepval Memorial, Pier and Face, 3 A and 3 D.

Robson, George, 3/8820, Private. KIA. Born in and a resident of Guisborough. Enlisted in Middlesbrough. Age 28. Buried in Bancourt British Cemetery in grave III. D. 9.

Rudge, Reginald Theodore, Second Lieutenant. KIA. Commemorated on Thiepval Memorial, Pier and Face, 3 A and 3 D.

Smith, John, 10063, Corporal. KIA. Born in Harome, Helmsley, Yorks and enlisted in Scarborough. Buried in London Cemetery and Extension, Longeuval in grave 7. F. 20.

Townsend, James, 16016, Private. KIA. Born in and a resident of North Ormesby, Middlesbrough. Enlisted in Middlesbrough. Age 22. Son of Major W. and Mary J. Townsend, of 24 Harrison Street, North Ormesby. Commemorated on Thiepval Memorial, Pier and Face, 3 A and 3 D.

Ward, Edwin, 27953, Private. KIA. Born in Guisborough, Yorkshire, a resident of Yarm and enlisted in Stockton. Commemorated on Thiepval Memorial, Pier and Face, 3 A and 3 D.

Operation to take the Gunpits

6 November 1916

10th Notts & Derbys.

Fletcher, George H., 14297, Private. KIA. Born in and a resident of Ripley, Derbyshire. Enlisted in Derby.

Foster, Ernest Edward, 19820, Private. KIA. Born and enlisted in Chesterfield.

Orion Trench Operation.

7th East Yorks.

Appleby, Frank, 21925, Private. KIA. Born in and a resident of Partington, Yorkshire. Enlisted in Hull. Commemorated on Thiepval Memorial, Pier and Face 2 C.

Bailey, Joseph, 13053, Corporal. M.M. KIA. Born and enlisted in Sheffield. Age 25. Son of Philip and Mary Ann Bailey and husband of Jessie Bailey, 11/1 Pitsmore Road, Sheffield. Commemorated on Thiepval Memorial, Pier and Face 2 C.

Baker, Alfred, 10636, Private. KIA. A resident of Grimsby and enlisted in Hull. Commemorated on Thiepval Memorial, Pier and Face 2 C.

Barber, Frank Vivian, 30928, Private. KIA. Born and enlisted in Hull. Commemorated on Thiepval Memorial, Pier and Face 2 C.

Baron, James Herbert, 11756, Private. KIA. Born in Manchester and enlisted in Sheffield. Commemorated on Thiepval Memorial, Pier and Face 2 C.

Beany, William, 14805, Private. KIA. Born in Silksworth, County Durham and enlisted in Sheffield. Commemorated on Thiepval Memorial, Pier and Face 2 C.

Bell, Edward Rider, 30840, Private. KIA. Born in Preston and enlisted in Hull. Age 29. Son of Edward and Hannah Maria Bell, 25 Westminster Avenue, Holderness Road, Hull. Commemorated on Thiepval Memorial, Pier and Face 2 C.

Bradley, Joseph, 30855, Private. KIA. Born in Willerby, Yorkshire and enlisted in Hull. Age 18. Son of Mrs. Annie Marwood (Formerly Bradley), Commemorated on Thiepval Memorial, Pier and Face 2 C.

Baimbridge, George, 30848. Private. KIA. Born and enlisted in Hull.

Calvert, Harold, 30858, Private. KIA. Born and enlisted in Hull. Age 28. Son of George Calvert, 54 Alexandra Street, Hull and husband of Eliza Sibbie Smith (Formerly Calvert), 38 A, Oxford Street, Castle Road, Scarborough. Commemorated on Thiepval Memorial, Pier and Face 2 C.

Chipp, George, 13083, Private. KIA. Born in Whitechapel, Middlesex and enlisted in Brierley, Yorkshire. Commemorated on Thiepval Memorial, Pier and Face 2 C.

Cooper, Thomas Frederick, 11852, Lance Corporal. KIA. Born in Walkley, Yorkshire and enlisted in Sheffield. Age 25. Son of William and Sarah Ann Cooper and husband of Martha Stones (formerly Cooper), 45 Channing Street, Walkley, Sheffield. Buried in Bancourt British Cemetery in grave, IV. J. 1.

Croft, Frederick Robert, 30863, Private. KIA. Born and enlisted in Hull. A resident of Scarborough. Commemorated on Thiepval Memorial, Pier and Face 2 C.

Cummings, Donald Archibald, 10904, Private. KIA. Born and enlisted in Hull. Age 36. Son of the Hugh and Joanna Cummings. Commemorated on Thiepval Memorial, Pier and Face 2 C.

Davis, Thomas, 13/1421. Private. KIA. Born in Sunderland and enlisted in Hull. Buried in A. I. F. Burial Ground, Flers in grave, IV. H. 10.

Drew, Frederick William, Second Lieutenant. KIA. Age 33. Attached to the 7th Battalion from the 9th Battalion. Son of Mrs. Elizabeth Drew of Bristol. Husband of Isabel Drew of 'Idene', Sandford Road, Mapperly, Nottingham. Recorded as an 'Old Colstonian'. Commemorated on Thiepval Memorial, Pier and Face 2 C.

Eastman, William Henry, 10980, Private. KIA. Born and enlisted in Hull. Age 24. Son of William Henry and Esther Eastman, 17 Barmston Street, Hull. Commemorated on Thiepval Memorial, Pier and Face 2 C.

Edson, James Frederick, 10/1095, Private. KIA. Born and enlisted in Hull. Age 26. Son of Charles H. and Louisa A. Edson, 4, Heaton Street, Brampton, Chesterfield, Derbyshire. Husband of Gertrude A. Edson. Commemorated on Thiepval Memorial, Pier and Face 2 C.

Edwards, Charles Walter, 34250, Private. KIA. Born in Nunhead, Surrey and a resident of Minehead, Somerset. Enlisted at Woolwich. Age 23. Son of Charles Walter and Katherine Edwards of Nunhead. Husband of Caroline Louisa Eacott, 41, Catesby Street, Rodney Road, Walworth, London. Buried in Bienvillers Military cemetery in grave XVIII. K. 8.

Foster, John William, 23216, Private. KIA. Born in Warham, Yorkshire and a resident of Driffield. Enlisted in Bainton. Commemorated on Thiepval Memorial, Pier and Face 2 C.

Foster, Robert Henderson, 14474, Corporal. D.C.M. KIA. Born and enlisted in Sunderland. Age 29. Son of Robert Henderson Foster and husband of Mary Arm Florence Searle (formerly Foster), 32, Sordey Street, Hendon, Sunderland. Commemorated on Thiepval Memorial, Pier and Face 2 C.

Frary, Charles, 23675, Private. KIA. Born and enlisted in Hull. Age 36. Husband of Ethel H. Frary, 13, Floral Avenue, Edinburgh Street, Hessle Road, Hull. Commemorated on Thiepval Memorial, Pier and Face 2 C.

Gardiner, Robert, 30869, Private. KIA. Born in Skirlaugh, Yorkshire and a resident of New Ellerby. Enlisted in Hull. Age 26. Son of Daniel and Anna Gardiner, Railway Cottages, Ellerby, Skirlaugh. Commemorated on Thiepval Memorial, Pier and Face 2 C.

Hanney, John, 21011, (CWGC records the number as 21001). Private. KIA. Born and enlisted in Hull. Commemorated on Thiepval Memorial, Pier and Face 2 C.

Helm, Arthur, 24888, Private. KIA. Born and enlisted in Hull. Commemorated on Thiepval Memorial, Pier and Face 2 C.

Hodkin, Harry, 13249, Private. KIA. Born and enlisted in Sheffield. Commemorated on Thiepval Memorial, Pier and Face 2 C.

Jackling, George, 22789, Private. KIA. Born in Brigg, Lincolnshire and enlisted in Hull. Commemorated on Thiepval Memorial, Pier and Face 2 C.

Johnson, George Henry, 22789, Corporal. KIA. Born in and a resident of Chatham. Enlisted in Hull.

Kelly, Jasper, 12638, Private. KIA. Born and enlisted in Hull. Age 35. The son of Daniel and Jane Kelly, 16 Bowers Terrace, Waterloo Street, Hull.

Kent, William, 17638, Private. KIA. Born in Dublin and a resident of Fencehouse. Enlisted at Shiney Row, County Durham. Age 20. Son of William and Jane Kent, 1, Wardroppers Cottage, Old Penshaw, Philadelphia, County Durham.

Langstaffe, Arthur Hudson, 19687, Private. KIA. Born in Leeds and a resident of St. Pancras. Enlisted at Marylebone. Commemorated on Thiepval Memorial, Pier and Face 2 C.

Major, Cyril Bisdee, Second Lieutenant. KIA. Age 19. Son of Dr. A. C. Major and Mrs. K. Major of Procter, British Columbia. Commemorated on Thiepval Memorial, Pier and Face 2 C.

Mason, William, 25385, Private. KIA. Born in Coalpool and enlisted in Walsall. Age 21. Son of William and Fanny Mason, Harden Road, Leamore, Walsall, Staffordshire. Commemorated on Thiepval Memorial, Pier and Face 2 C.

Naylor, George, 12676, Lance Corporal. KIA. Born and enlisted in Attercliffe, York. Son of Mr. D. J. Naylor, 43, Ronald Road, Darnall, Sheffield. Buried in Bancourt British Cemetery in grave IV. F. 6.

Nickolay, Joseph, 10102, Corporal. KIA. Born in and a resident of Westminster. Enlisted in Bury. Commemorated on Thiepval Memorial, Pier and Face 2 C.

Parkin, Willie, 3/7135, Lance Corporal. KIA. Born and enlisted in Sheffield. Commemorated on Thiepval Memorial, Pier and Face 2 C.

Platt, Harold, 30900, Private. C Company. KIA. Born and enlisted in Hull. Age 22. Son of William Robert and Mary A. Platt, Hessle, Yorkshire. Commemorated on Thiepval Memorial, Pier and Face 2 C.

Robinson, Thomas, 22580, Private. KIA. Born and enlisted in Hull. Commemorated on Thiepval Memorial, Pier and Face 2 C.

Sales, John William, 22498, Lance Corporal. KIA. Born and enlisted in Hull. Commemorated on Thiepval Memorial, Pier and Face 2 C.

Smirthwaite, John William, 15298, Private. KIA. Born and enlisted in Bishop Auckland. Commemorated on Thiepval Memorial, Pier and Face 2 C.

Smith, Wallis, 12295, Acting Lance Sergeant. C Company. KIA. Born and enlisted in Bradford. Age 20. Son of Mr. T and Mrs H. M. Smith. Commemorated on Thiepval Memorial, Pier and Face 2 C.

Stead, Frank William, 22849, Private. KIA. Born in Sharleston, Yorkshire and enlisted in Hull. Age 33. Son of Walter and Mary J. Stead, 89, Victoria Avenue, Hull. Commemorated on Thiepval Memorial, Pier and Face 2 C.

Steels, John, 30914, Private. KIA. Born in Sharleston, Yorkshire and enlisted in Hull. Age 21. Son of Mrs. Steels, 8, Liverpool Street, Hessle Road, Hull, Buried in Guards Cemetery, Lesboeufs in grave, V. U. 10.

Swales, Walter, 34264, Private. KIA. Born in Knottingley, Yorkshire and enlisted in Normanton. Commemorated on Thiepval Memorial, Pier and Face 2 C.

Taylor, Henry, 16738, Lance Corporal. KIA. Born and enlisted in Hull. Commemorated on Thiepval Memorial, Pier and Face 2 C.

Taylor, Herbert Edward, 30915, Private. KIA. Born in and a resident of Beverley. Enlisted in Hull. Commemorated on Thiepval Memorial, Pier and Face 2 C.

Wall, William, 12019, Private. KIA. Born and enlisted in Sheffield. Commemorated on Thiepval Memorial, Pier and Face 2 C.

Waudby, Alfred Neaves, 30919, Private. KIA. Born in and a resident of North Ferriby, Yorkshire. Enlisted in Hull. Age 19. Son of Henry and Lizzie Waudby, 6, Church Cottages, North Ferriby, Yorkshire. Commemorated on Thiepval Memorial, Pier and Face 2 C.

Wilkinson, William, 30924, Private. KIA. Born and enlisted in Hull. Age 20. Son of William and Jane Wilkinson, Seaton, Hull. Commemorated on Thiepval Memorial, Pier and Face 2 C.

Wilks, John William, 11135, Corporal. KIA. Born and enlisted in Hull. Commemorated on Thiepval Memorial, Pier and Face 2 C.

8 November 1916

6th Dorsets.

Agelasto, August, Lieutenant, M.C. KIA. Originally of 1st Battalion and attached to the 6th Battalion. Mentioned in Despatches, 1 July 1916. Age 28. Of Greek descent. Son of Stephen and Caterina Agelasto, 185, Gloucester Terrace, Hyde Park, London. Buried Guards' Cemetery Les Boeufs in grave, X. X. 9.

25 November 1916

10th Notts & Derbys

Randle, W. H., Private. Shot at dawn for desertion. Pardoned, 2006. Formerly in the 9th Notts & Derbys and a Gallipoli veteran. Born on Wollaton Street Hucknall, Nottinghamshire. The son of William Henry & Harriett Randle of 26, Vale Drive, Shirebrook, Nottinghamshire. Buried in Cavillon Communal Cemetery in the northwest corner.

8 December 1916

7th Borders

Simpson, John Watt, Second Lieutenant. KIA, (the battalion war diary records killed in an accident on 9 December, the Medal Index Card records KIA on 8 December, *Soldiers Died in the Great War* records killed on 8 December). Probably killed in a Mortar accident. A Kitchener Volunteer and formerly, Rifleman B3213, 8th Rifle Brigade. Son of James and Louisa Henderson Simpson of North Bank House, Portree, Skye. Buried in Vaux-En-Amienois Communal Cemetery in grave A. 4.

9 December 1916

7th Yorks.

Poole, Harry, Rifleman, 3/8534. Shot at dawn for desertion. Pardoned, 2006. Son of Mr. A. Poole, of 9, Bernard Street, Sheffield. Buried in Cavillon Communal Cemetery in the northwest corner.

16 December 1916

8th South Staffords

Cotterell, Frederic Hampson, Lieutenant. DOW after a trench mortar accident, age 27. Son of Mr. F. J. Cotterell of "East View", Sutton Road, Walsall, Staffordshire. Buried in St. Pierre Cemetery, Amiens in grave V. B. 3.

9 January 1917

Soames, Gilbert Horsman, Major (formerly Temporary Lieutenant-Colonel, 10th West Yorks). 1st West Yorks. KIA. Age 37. The son of Arthur W. Soames, M.P. Husband of Rose Eveline Soames of 2, Petersham Place, Gloucester Road, South Kensington. Buried in Cambrin Churchyard Extension in grave T. 18.

3 May 1917

Getty, James Houghton, Captain. 7th Lincolns, transferred to 12th Manchesters. Killed in action. Family lived at 16, Dunbar Road, Bournemouth. Commemorated on Arras Memorial, Bay 4.

28 January 1918

Kay, S. B., Captain. 7th Yorks and R.F.C. Died of Wounds. Buried in Leeds (Lawnswood) Cemetery and is one of 88 burials with no grave marker. He is commemorated on Screen Wall T. 42.

4 or 5 April 1918.[502]

Clive, Percy Archer, Lieutenant-Colonel, M.P., D.S.O., Legion of Honour, Croix de Guerre, (1st Grenadier Guards and former C.O. of the 7th East Yorks), C. O. of the 1/5th Lancashire Fusiliers. Member of Parliament for Herefordshire. KIA. Age 35. Son of Charles Meysey Bolton Clive and the Lady Catherine. Husband of Alice Muriel Clive. Commemorated on Arras Memorial.

14 or 15 October 1918.[503]

Lundie, Robert Charles, Major, D.S.O., 93rd Field Company, R.E. KIA. Age 33. Son of R. A. Lundie, M.B., C.M., F.R.C.E., and Annie Sarah Lundie of 24 Omidale Terrace, Edinburgh. Home address given as Mrs. R. B. Watson, 7, Hendon Lane, Finchley. Buried in Caudry British Cemetery in grave II. F. 6.

---

[502] The Commonwealth War Graves Commission records his death on 4 April and *Soldiers Died in the Great War 1914 – 1918* records it as 5 April.

[503] The Commonwealth War Graves Commission records his death on 14 October and *Soldiers Died in the Great War 1914 – 1918* records it as 15 October.

Bibliography

Published Works

A Hilliard Atteridge, *History of the 17th (Northern) Division*, (Robert Maclehose & Co. Ltd, 1929)

W. N. Hoyte & M. T. F. J. McNeela (Ed), *10th (S) Battalion The Sherwood Foresters, The History Of The Battalion During The Great War*, (Originally written shortly after the war's end. First published, Naval & Military Press, 2003)

G. O' Hanlon, *A Plain History of the Sixth (Service) Battalion, The Dorsetshire Regiment 1914 – 1919, in The History of the Dorsetshire Regiment 1914 – 1919*. Part three, the Service Battalions. (First published, Henry Ling, Ltd, 1932. Re-printed by Naval & Military Press)

R. Kipling, *The Irish Guards in the Great War*, Volume II, (First published 1923).

W. Osborne, *A History Of The 10th Battalion The Notts & Derbys, Volume Two, The Bluff To The Somme 1916*. (First published, Salient Books, 2011).

W. Miles, *Official History Of The Great War, Military Operations France and Belgium, 1916, Vol II*, (First published, 1938. Re-printed by the Imperial War Museum and the Battery Press, 1992).

G. Sheffield & J. Bourne, (Eds), *Douglas Haig War Diaries and Letters 1914 – 1918*, (BCA, 2005).

R. Prior & T. Wilson, *Command on the Western Front, The Military Career of Sir Henry Rawlinson 1914 – 1918*, (Blackwell Publishers, 1992. Re-printed, Pen & Sword, 2004).

G. S. Duncan, *Douglas Haig As I Knew Him,* (George Allen and Unwin Ltd, First published, 1966).

M. Gilvary, *History Of The 7th Service Battalion The York And Lancaster Regiment (Pioneers) 1914 -1919.* (The Talbot Press, Ltd, 1921)

S. Rogerson, *Twelve Days On The Somme, A Memoir of the Trenches, 1916*, (First published 1933, Re-published, Greenhill Books, 2006)

C. P. Blacker & J. Blacker (Ed), *Have You Forgotten Yet? The First World War Memoirs of C. P. Blacker, MC, GM,* (First published, Leo Cooper, 2000. Re-published, Pen & Sword, 2015)

C. Carrington, *Soldier From The Wars Returning,* (First published, Hutchinson & Co, 1965. Republished, Pen & Sword 2006 & 2015)

W. Osborne, Quadrangles, The 17th (Northern) Division On The Somme, 6 – 11 July 1916, (Salient Books, 2010).

A. M. Henniker, *Transportation On The Western Front,* (First published, H.M.S.O, 1933. Re-printed Imperial War Museum and Naval & Military Press, 2009).

E. A, Pratt, *British Railways and The Great War, Organisation, Efforts, Difficulties and Achievements,* Vol I & II, (London, Selwyn and Blount, Ltd, 1921).

Unpublished Works, Memoirs and Diaries

Personal diary of Lieutenant-Colonel Fife held at the Green Howards Museum, Richmond.

Imperial War Museum (IWM): Unpublished papers Captain B. C. Mozley, D.S.O. 01/48/1.

Imperial War Museum (IWM): Unpublished papers, Corporal Eric H. Harlow, M.M. 03/15/1.

Imperial War Museum (IWM): Unpublished papers of Sapper and later Colonel, F. Palmer Cook, O.B.E., T.D. 81/44/1.

War Diaries

TNA: PRO. WO 95/360. War Diary, Third Army, 1916.

TNA: PRO. WO 95/805. War Diary, VII Corps, 1916.

TNA: PRO. WO 95/911. War Diary, XIV Corps, 1916.

TNA: PRO. WO 95/1981. War Diary, 17th Division, 1916.

TNA: PRO. WO 95/1986. War Diary, Adjutant & Quartermaster General, 1916.

TNA: PRO. WO 95/1989. War Diary, A.D.M.S., 1916.

TNA: PRO. WO 95/1990. War Diary, A.D.V.S., 1916.

TNA: PRO. WO 95/1992. War Diary, 17th Divisional Ammunition Column, 1916.

TNA: PRO. WO 95/1997. War Diary, 29th Mobile Veterinary Section, 1916.

TNA: PRO. WO 95/1994. War Diary, 17th Signal Company, 1916.

TNA: PRO. WO 95/1997. War Diary, 34th Sanitary Section, 1916.

TNA: PRO. WO 95/1993. War Diary, 78th Field Company, R.E., 1916.

TNA: PRO. WO 95/1993. War Diary, 93rd Field Company R.E., 1916.

TNA: PRO. WO 95/1998. War Diary, 50th Brigade, 1916.

TNA: PRO. WO 95/2005. War Diary, 51st Brigade, 1916.

TNA: PRO. WO95/2006. War Diary, 52nd Brigade, 1916.

TNA: PRO. WO 95/1996. War Diaries, 51st, Field Ambulance, 1916.

TNA: PRO. WO 95/1996. War Diaries, 52nd Field Ambulances, 1916.

TNA: PRO. WO 95/1996. War Diary, 53rd Field Ambulance, 1916.

TNA: PRO. WO 95/2004. War Diary, 50th Brigade Machine Gun Company, 1916.

TNA: PRO. WO 95/2014. War Diary, 52nd Brigade Machine Gun Company, 1916.

TNA: PRO. WO 95/2004. War Diary, 7th Yorks, 1916.

TNA: PRO. WO 95/2008. War Diary, 7th Borders, 1916.

TNA: PRO. WO 95/2007. War Diary, 7th Lincolns, 1916.

TNA: PRO. WO95/2012. War Diary, 10th Lancashire Fusiliers, 1916.

TNA: PRO. WO 95/2014. War Diary, 9th Duke of Wellingtons, West Riding Regiment, 1916.

TNA: PRO. WO 95/2004. War Diary, 10th West Yorks, 1916.

TNA: PRO. WO 95/2002. War Diary, 7th East Yorks, 1916.

TNA: PRO. WO 95/2007. War Diary, 8th South Staffords, 1916.

TNA: PRO WO 95/2000. War Diary, 6th Dorsets, 1916.

TNA: PRO. WO95/2012. War Diary, 10th Lancashire Fusiliers, 1916.

TNA: PRO. WO 95/2013. War Diary, 9th Northumberland Fusiliers, 1916.

TNA: PRO. WO 95/2012. War Diary, 12th Manchesters, 1916.

TNA: PRO. WO95/1618. War Diary, 1st West Yorks, 1916 & 1917.

TNA: PRO. WO 95/2694. War Diary, 1/6th Notts & Derbys, 1916.

Electronic Sources

Soldiers Died In The Great War, 1914 – 1918.

Ancestry.com

Index

Mairis, G. B. de, Lieutenant-Colonel, 117, 129

Major, Second Lieutenant, Cyril Bisdee, 102

Mametz Village, 42

Mametz Wood, 136, 178

Mansell Camp, 42, 46

Mansell Copse, 42, 46, 64

Matthews, Captain, E. R., 53

Meaulte, 42, 55, 64, 143

Merryweather, Second Lieutenant, R. H., 94

Metcalfe, Lieutenant-Colonel, 24, 129

Metcalf, Second Lieutenant, 104

Middlehurst, Private, Moses, 45

Mild Trench, 97, 99, 147

Minden Post, 45-6, 51, 68

Misty Trench, 76, 85, 89-1, 93

Molliens en Vidames, 54, 112, 118

Montauban, 41, 43, 72

Moore, Captain J., 103

Morgan, Second Lieutenant, H. L., 85-7

Morlancourt, 47

Moulton-Barrett, Major, A. L., 129

Mozley, Captain, Bernard C., 18, 20-3, 28-9, 35, 41-4, 56-7, 69-70, 72-3, 76,-83, 111-12, 117-18, 124, 129-36, 164

Nasmith, Captain, Arthur Plater, 86, 87, 89

Neale, Major, W. W. R., 60-1, 65, 66, 74

Neale, Private, H, 60-1, 65-6, 74

Nephritis, 62

Nicholson, Lieutenant-Colonel, Octavius Henry Lothian, 31, 68, 122

Nissen Huts, 129

Orion Trench, 97, 99-104, 106, 149, 152

Peronne, 41

Poole, Rifleman, Harry, 35, 126, 159

Push Tubes, 29

Quadrangle Support Trench, 17, 136, 178

Radford, Captain, Basil Hallam, 23

Randle, Private, William Henry, 123, 158

Rawlinson, General, Sir Henry, 34-5, 37, 40, 95, 97, 110, 137, 163

Reynolds, Private, S. Walter, 49

Robertson, Lieutenant,, 5, 18, 26, 27, 28, 29, 55, 101, 105, 110-12, 114, 116, 119-20, 131, 134, 137

Robertson, Major-General, Philip Rynd, 5, 18, 26-8, 29, 55, 101, 105, 110-12, 114, 116, 119-20, 131, 134, 137

Robinson, Second Lieutenant, J. E., 94, 144, 146, 157

Rogerson, Captain, Sidney, 44, 82, 163

Rubella, 62

Rudge, Second Lieutenant, Reginald Theodore, 105, 151

Rum, 69

Sailly-Laurette, 47

Sailly-le-Sec, 47

Sandpits Camp, 42

Simner, P. R., Major, 33, 117, 129

Simpson, Second Lieutenant, J. W., 121-2, 159

Snow, Lieutenant-General, Sir Thomas D'Oyly, 24, 26, 28

Soames, Lieutenant-Colonel, Gilbert Horsman,, 57, 77, 114-18, 131, 160

Somme, area, 3, 7, 9, 10, 15, 16, 19, 23, 26, 30, 33-6, 38-42, 44, 46, 48-9, 51, 53-4, 58, 66, 71-3, 82, 96,

More about the
17th (Northern) Division

The following titles by the same author are available from Salient Books:

Quadrangles
The 17th (Northern) Division on the Somme, 6–11 July 1916

The story of the Battle of the Somme was not just about one day in July. Not every unit was 'strung up on the wire' on the first day of the battle and the attack was not totally stalled. There had been horrendous casualties but on the right flank, since 1 July, the British Army was advancing against a withdrawing enemy.

The conditions around Quadrangle Trench and Quadrangle Support Trench were dreadful, the rain was torrential and the mud deep. This section of the line, between Mametz Wood and Contalmaison was the scene of bitter fighting and heavy losses on both sides. Despite the weather, severed communications, hopeless piecemeal attacks and having to fight uphill, the 17th (Northern) Division did what it was ordered to do. The battalions pushed on and took their objectives.

This was the 17th (Northern) Division's first tour of duty in the Somme battle. The account has been pieced together using War Diaries from The National Archive and unpublished papers from the Imperial War Museum. This is the beginning of the story of a Kitchener Division on the Somme.

Delville Wood
The 17th (Northern) Division on the Somme, 1–14 August 1916

The 17th (Northern) Division comprised the 6th Dorsets, 7th Green Howards, 7th East Yorks, 10th West Yorks, 7th Borders, 7th Lincolns, 8th South Staffords, 10th Notts & Derbys, 9th Duke of Wellington's, 9th Northumberland Fusiliers and the 12th Manchesters.

For two weeks in August 1916 the Division and its support units held the line in the burning ruins of Longueval and the splintered remains of Delville Wood.

Pounded by the guns of both sides the Division, newly reinforced by green, untrained troops after the fighting of early July, was called upon to hold the line and assault well defended enemy positions.

Lightning Source UK Ltd.
Milton Keynes UK
UKHW02f0114110118
315901UK00005B/89/P